Eva Brewster was born in 1922 to a wealthy family in Berlin. Her father died shortly after being stripped of his property by the Nazis. At the age of sixteen, Eva married Freddy Raphael and they had a daughter, Reha. In 1943 the family was sent to the concentration camps at Auschwitz and Birkenau, which only Eva and her mother survived.

After the war, Eva remarried and lived in Africa, England, and Scotland before settling in southern Alberta with her husband and daughter. She has become well known for her determined defence of personal rights and freedoms. For twelve years, she wrote a column for the *Lethbridge Herald*, that allowed her to express views on democracy, intolerance, and racial prejudice. Friends persuaded her to revise for publication the memoirs of the concentration camp that she wrote shortly after the war, and her experience became immediately relevant when a schoolteacher in southern Alberta was found teaching that the Holocaust is a hoax.

Eva Brewster has been involved in numerous writing and research projects. In 1976 she was chosen "Ms Chatelaine" and was a YWCA "Woman of the Year" in 1977. In recognition of her writing and her service to humanity, an honorary Doctor of Laws degree was awarded to her by the University of Lethbridge in 1986.

VANISHED IN DARKNESS

An Auschwitz Memoir

Eva Brewster

NeWest Press   Edmonton

Copyright ©1986 Eva Brewster

Canadian Cataloguing in Publication Data

Brewster, Eva, 1923-

Vanished in darkness

ISBN 0-920897-06-1

1. Brewster, Eva, 1923-   2. Auschwitz (Poland: Concentration camp).   3. Holocaust, Jewish (1939-1945) - Personal narratives.   4. World War, 1939-1945 - Prisoners and prisons, German.   I. Title.

D805.P7B74 1986   940.54'72'430924   C86-091530-1

Credits

Cover design: Bob Robertson
Printing and binding: Hignell Printers, Winnipeg

Financial Assistance

Alberta Culture
The Canada Council

This publication was made possible by the generous assistance of The Alberta Foundation for the Literary Arts.

NeWest Publishers Ltd.
Suite 204, 8631 - 109 Street
Edmonton, Alberta, Canada   T6G 1E8

Acknowledgments

Neither my travels nor my writing would have been possible without my husband's unwavering support. The antithesis of the "mean" Scotsman, he has given me more than I ever dreamed of throughout our married life. For nearly forty years, he has been at the receiving end of, and wakened me up from, my recurring violent nightmares to reassure me that I could stop fighting and that I was safe with him. On October 18, 1986, shortly before this edition of my book was to be published, he died peacefully, after a long battle with heart and kidney failure, in his sleep. If I cry, I cry for myself and for the need to face the ongoing battle for human rights and dignity alone; but he left me a legacy of renewed strength and trust in humanity, love and decency.

To Cleo Mowers, retired publisher of the *Lethbridge Herald,* I owe a debt of gratitude. He never ceased to encourage and promote my journalistic career. When in July, 1979, our only son died at age twenty-four in a motor-bike accident and all hope and sunshine had gone out of my life once again, he insisted that I had an obligation to carry on. He persuaded me that, with my writing, I still had something worthwhile and necessary to contribute to our society in general and to a new generation in particular.

My sincere thanks to Doug Walker, former Editorial page Editor of the *Lethbridge Herald,* for his interest, involvement and efforts to publish my weekly column over twelve years.

I also wish to thank Joanne Helmer for her generous help in correcting and attempting to edit this story. She encouraged me—perhaps against my better judgment—to relive the most tragic era of this century. After long and tiring days of newspaper work, she sacrificed untold free hours to my manuscript for no better reason than her conviction that "everybody must read this book."

My husband's secretary, Violet Thielen, deserves a grateful acknowledgment for helping to type the original manuscript after spending her working days in a busy government office.

The Canada Council also helped with the development of my book by giving a generous grant to Andy Ogle, the former City Editor of the *Lethbridge Herald*. This enabled him to devote himself full time to the completion of, and necessary changes in, my original manuscript.

Last, but by no means least, my sincere thanks to Andy Ogle for the hardest job of all—the editing of the manuscript—and his contributions of Prologue and Epilogue, which may add to the reader's understanding of my motivation for writing this story at this time. Long before he received a Canada Council grant to complete his editorial efforts, he spent his own time and money on repeated visits to my remote home in Coutts to interview me because he, too, believed that the book "should be published."

Prologue

by Andrew Ogle

In our comfortable, comfort-loving age, it is difficult for anyone, but especially for young people who have known no other life, to imagine what life in Hitler's Germany was like for a teen-ager who also happened to be Jewish. Eva Brewster, married at sixteen, knew the horrors of Auschwitz where she lost her first child and young husband in the gas chambers neo-Nazis and other anti-Semites now claim never existed. She spent the last of her teenage years in that hell on earth and was one of only seven survivors of a transport of one thousand young people who entered it with her.

She first wrote about her experience in Auschwitz as a form of therapy, a way of coming to grips with the pain and suffering of those years. "Immediately after the war," she relates, "people used to ask me over a cup of coffee what it was really like to be a prisoner of the Nazis. Initially, I tried to tell them a little about our ordeals. They'd stare at me as though I were a visitor from a strange planet and say 'How terrible! Can I have another piece of cake please?' So I never talked about my experiences again and wrote them down instead, which somehow seemed to help me preserve my sanity.

"For years, the manuscript remained locked up in a drawer like a dark, oppressive secret. Later, married again, I told myself that a lot of water had been flowing under the bridges of the world since the dark days of the "Thousand Year Reich." Together with my children, a new generation was growing up and I didn't want to burden them with the horrors I had seen. In short, I repeated my parents' mistakes. Sheltering my children behind a solid wall of love, tenderness and material advantages, I tried in vain to protect them from hurt."

Even with the decision made to write the book, Eva found the task difficult to face and that led her to use the name Daniella Raphael even though she was describing her own life. Daniella was the name given her in the Resistance which she had joined during the war. Raphael was her first married name. "The only way I could bring myself to relive that period," she says, "was by thinking of Daniella as another person in another life and on a different continent."

VANISHED
IN DARKNESS

Chapter 1

"Daniella Raphael!" A grey-haired prison wardress with a kind face and sad, old eyes called me from contemplation of the tiny piece of blue sky that could be seen through the high, heavily-barred window.

"Daniella," she repeated, "will you follow me to my office to sign your release papers? I won't keep you long and you can go home as soon as you like. Unless," she added with a smile, "you would rather have some lunch before you go?"

I was speechless. My heart missed a beat and then started racing. I looked at the four girls who had shared the cell with me and saw their startled, doubtful expression. Nobody in my position had ever been released from jail once the Nazis had them in their clutches. Besides, where was I to go? My husband was a prisoner and news had reached me that my mother-in-law had been deported and her house requisitioned. My mind was in such a turmoil that I almost forgot my own mother, who was still nursing the remnants of a fast-dwindling community in the Jewish hospital in East Berlin. Of course, I could go to her.

"Don't look so thunderstruck, girl, and come with me," said the wardress. "To look at you, one might think you were loath to leave this comfortable place. Come on child, you and your type don't belong here. Somebody seems to have realized a mistake has been made."

I followed her to her bare little office, too excited to say goodbye to my fellow prisoners. Right enough, there was my file on her desk. My name was on it, but the details had been left blank. I began to understand why the wardress thought I had been arrested by mistake. I was young, barely 20 years old, and hope surged up inside me like a song.

The wardress handed me my pen and the money which had been taken from me when I had been arrested. I signed the release papers; she shook hands with me and, smiling, warned me to keep away from prison in future. She then rang the bell and a young woman in uniform came in to take me to the gate and show me where to get a bus. The policewoman took me past innumerable cells and down staircase after staircase into the yard and through the slowly opening iron gates.

I remember little about this prison in Moabit, Berlin, the last of eleven. All I recollect is the warm sun and the sweet scent and promise of spring in the air. I told the girl I knew my way about Berlin and asked her to leave me. All I wanted was to stand still and savor the sunlight and the freedom after three months' imprisonment.

And so I stood, leaning against a tree, taking deep breaths of fresh air, completely and childishly happy. I did not contemplate my next move but cast my mind back over the past few months. This was the beginning of April, 1943. It seemed so long, long ago since I had seen my child the last time.

Chapter 2

My little Reha was only a baby when I was forced to work in a factory and to leave her in a day-care centre. I had an hour's journey each way to and from work. Reha was the first child at the centre in the morning and the last to be collected at night. I remember her forlorn little figure, sitting half asleep in a tiny chair in the huge, deserted play-room, generally dressed to go out, her coat buttoned up and her bonnet the wrong way round on her dark little head.

I remember the delighted shriek when she saw me at last and how I wrapped her up and took her round the shops in her stroller to buy a little food. In winter it was pitch dark. Jews were no longer given scarce milk, butter, eggs or fruit. Sometimes, a kind woman in a fruit shop would wrap up a few apples if nobody was around but, if Reha saw this, she would cry all the way home for me to give her one. I could not risk letting her eat an apple in the street. We had to wear a large yellow star with "JEW" printed across it, and an apple or a piece of chocolate seen in the hand of a Jewish child had been the excuse for deportation of whole families.

One could get all the forbidden things in the black market at terrific prices but our bank accounts were blocked and we had to live on the pay-packets from the factory. Slave labor wages were barely enough to pay for rent and for the rationed food allotted to us.

My husband occasionally did some private work. Carpentry was his hobby and sometimes he sold a bookshelf, a cabinet, or a set of small tables. Then, for a week or so, we had plenty to eat and Reha got a taste of

chocolate, bananas or oranges. Of course, when such luxuries were scarce she would beg me for them. It just about
broke my heart if there was nothing but mashed potatoes
and some nondescript soup for her supper.

All this was bearable when we still lived in our comfortable home. At least we were together in the evenings.
My husband played with the baby, bathed her and put her
to bed while I cooked our evening meal, such as it was,
swept and cleaned the house and did our washing and iron-
ing. After the child was in bed and the essential chores
done, we could still sit together for an hour or two and talk
of the future and what we would do when the Nazis were
thrown out and the war over. Or, if we were too tired to
talk, we would listen to records or a concert or a play on
the radio, or just read.

Even that short spell of small joys and comparative
comfort soon came to an end. More and more people were
being arrested for trivial or fictitious reasons. Whole families were deported, nobody knew where. Old and sick people were dragged out of their beds to police stations and
then vanished. My mother told me of the many, many old
people who attempted suicide. Often their attempts were
unsuccessful and they were taken to hospital to be nursed
back to health only to be arrested and sent to an unknown,
terrifying destiny. My mother, who was a senior sister on
the emergency ward, chose not to nurse them back to life.
They passed out peacefully while she sat at their side.
Holding frail, tired hands, she talked to them in her sweet,
soft voice of the past and of their children, who were
perhaps safely abroad. She talked to them until the drugs
they had taken took effect and the old people closed their
eyes, no longer afraid of the dark, holding her hand with a
tightening grip and, finally, relaxing into peaceful, eternal
sleep.

Then, one day she was told by a Gestapo man in

charge of sick prisoners at the hospital that a campaign was in preparation to evacuate all Jewish families with young children. As soon as my mother warned me, I decided to hide our child. We did not know what was in store for us but, whatever it was, I was not going to drag a baby into it. A friend, a Christian nurse, proposed to take Reha to her brother in East Prussia and tell him the baby's parents had been killed in an air raid on Berlin.

My mother-in-law vetoed the plan. She said we would all be shot if the Gestapo found out the child had disappeared. We were living in her house by that time as my parents' home had long since been requisitioned by the German Broadcasting Corporation. She was right, of course, but she did not stop to consider that we would probably be killed anyway. My husband backed her up and I decided I would have to leave them. He was so young and I wondered if he could keep a secret if he were tortured. We knew by then of the Gestapo methods of wringing secrets from their suspects and I wanted my husband to be able to swear he knew nothing of the whereabouts of his little daughter. Since I had to leave the house anyway, I was going to take no risks. I explained my motives and he agreed to a divorce, which was much easier than I had thought. We found one of his ex-girlfriends more than willing to spend a night with him and I got a divorce on the grounds of desertion and adultery. After that I moved with Reha into a rented apartment in a house belonging to another Jewish family.

The last two weeks with my child were agony. I had not dared to stay away from work in case the Gestapo became suspicious and arrested me before I got the chance to hide our little girl. The date for her departure was fixed and I knew I would soon see her for the last time. I rushed home at night as fast as I could and often wondered what went on inside that little head when I got to her. She was more affectionate than she had ever been before, kissed and hugged me almost as though I were the child. She never asked for her Daddy or why we had left home for that chilly, impersonal room. Yet she loved her father dearly.

Once more I took her to see him on his twenty-second birthday. We went after dark and sneaked in through the back door. Reha had seen me wrap a present for him and so she had decided to take her most valued possession, a woolly little lamb that had accompanied her everywhere. She handed it to her father and said, "Happy Birthday, Daddy." But the tears in her eyes emphasized more than anything else that there was nothing happy about it. We only stayed for half an hour and before we left my husband put his arms around me. For the first time since I left him, I broke down and cried, quite unable to control myself. Suddenly I felt a light tug on my coat and the little voice said, "Don't cry, Mummy. I'm going to take my lamb back so we won't be so lonely. You don't mind, Daddy, do you?" She tucked her toy under her arm and sneaked out of the door without looking up, guilt and bad conscience personified in a two and a half-year-old child.

Margaret, the Christian nurse, was going to take an early train to East Prussia and I was to meet her with Reha just after midnight at the station where trains left for the east, about a 45-minute walk from my apartment. I had given Reha sleeping pills hoping she would not notice anything until she was on the train. But I was ignorant in those days, and in order to spare my mother's feelings had not discussed this with her. I thought if I gave Reha twice the prescribed dose she would sleep sounder. The overdose had exactly the opposite effect. She cried and cried, became quite hysterical, and by 10 p.m. was still wide awake, feverish and restless and I was shaken and at my wits' end. About 11 p.m. she was sick, had a drink of water, and at last fell into a deep, exhausted sleep.

I did not dress her, wrapped her in three thick blankets, tucked her little lamb in as well and crept out of the house. It was a dark night, icy cold and windy but I did not dare take a taxi for fear of drawing attention to us. So I walked. The sleeping child grew heavier and heavier in my arms but this dead weight and the icy wind I had to battle kept my mind off the imminent separation. At last I reached the corner opposite the station. There was no moon and it was so dark I did not see Margaret approaching. When she put her hand on my shoulder, I all but collapsed with fright. "It's all right, Daniella," she said, and the next moment she had taken the sleeping child from my arms and was gone. I tried to run after her, but she was already lost in the dark.

"I have not even kissed her, I have not even kissed her," was all that went through my agonized mind like a broken record as I slowly walked back to my apartment. I don't know how I got home that night. I remember waking up in the morning kneeling in front of the empty cot, my head buried in the small pillow. I was cold and stiff and lonelier than I have been in my life before or since.

Chapter 3

After Reha was gone, I was on the run, always in contact with the Resistance movement which I had quickly joined. This organization, to me, was nothing more than some Christian names, meetings with mysterious people in obscure pubs and street corners in Berlin or under the shade of the Munster of Strassbourg. Off and on, through Resistance contacts, meetings were arranged for my husband and me in equally obscure places. He too was trying to escape arrest, not knowing where he was going or what I was doing. Neither of us stayed for more than a night in any one place and often it was very difficult to find a safe shelter. It would have been a comfort in those dark, cold winter nights to at least walk together, but even that was against Resistance rules and regulations. Within six months, I lost trace of his whereabouts altogether.

At the end of January, 1943, the Resistance dispatched me to Dornbirn, a small border village. I was given some documents—technical drawings of I know not what—for delivery to Switzerland. I had been told to lie low until my contact in Dornbirn turned up. His name was Peter and I was to obey his instructions until I was across the border. There, new contacts would meet me, receive the papers and return me to Germany. I was promised that on completion of three similar missions, I would be allowed to stay in Switzerland where my husband and child would join me.

At midnight of the 3rd of February, my train stopped in Dornbirn. It was a dark, cold night. Only two other passengers got out at the station, one a young man in fur coat and beaver hat, another in a skiing outfit. They left from different compartments and went straight to the only exit of that little station. I waited till they were out of sight, then followed slowly, wondering where to "lie low" at this time of night. I need not have worried.The two men were waiting for me.

They identified themselves as Gestapo and then offered me the hospitality of the local police station. As each had taken one of my arms in an iron grip, there was no way I could refuse their invitation. At the police station they started to bombard me with questions.

I stuck to my fictitious past, drummed into me day and night during the long weeks of the Resistance briefing. The two Gestapo men were obviously beginners. When they saw no information was forthcoming, they proceeded to search me for identity cards and documents. I had the presence of mind to ask for a woman officer to search me. One could still cling to a moral code in an isolated frontier station. In a larger place, I would have been beaten for impudence and the men would have continued their search. However, the two complied with my demand and locked me in a coal cellar. A messenger was dispatched to rouse the female employed to search women tourists for Customs, while I began to look around for a suitable corner to dispose of my documents.

Barely had I begun, when the door creaked open and in came a uniformed police officer. In a loud voice, holding open the door, he said, "I'm in charge of this border station. Checking to see prisoners are accounted for." Then he shut the door and whispered, "I am Peter. Give me the papers, quickly!" He took the drawings, opened an iron gate leading from the coal cellar to the station's furnaces and burned them on the spot. He said that was all he could do for me at the moment, but he would see me again. "Stick to your story whatever happens," he warned, and with that he left.

Shortly afterwards, I was taken back to the office upstairs. A woman made me undress behind a screen and searched my clothes. Everything she found in my coat pockets she handed to the two officers. She tore open the lining of my coat, the hem of my skirt, belt and collar of my sweater, of course without results. I was then permitted to dress again and my captors called me over to their desks. In front of them were my make-up compact, the mirror torn out and splintered, my lipstick broken out of its case and crumpled, and my necklace unwound and partly broken with beads scattered all over the desk and floor.

"Madam," the older of the men said, "it would be in your interest to make a full confession. While we did not yet find what we were looking for, we did get your description and details of your despicable intentions from headquarters. If you refuse to make a statement, we shall charge you with spying, the intention to unlawfully cross the frontier into foreign territory and the contacting of enemy agents conspiring against the German Reich. You know the penalty for these crimes? We give you ten minutes to think it over."

My reply was that I could not confess to something I knew nothing about. Unless they could produce evidence that I was not the person shown in my passport, I had nothing more to say until they brought me to trial in an open court. I would then do my best to defend myself. That was a last and desperate attempt to bluff my way out of a bad situation. My guess that these two were inexperienced and had not yet been properly trained in methods of inquisition and torture proved correct.

Far from calling my bluff, they attempted to produce evidence in the form of a telegram which they handed to me. The headquarters of my Resistance organization, a business house at the Potsdamer Platz in Berlin, had been raided by the Gestapo and a few people had been arrested.

It appeared that, in order to save more important members, they had given the names and details of employment of some insignificant agents like myself who could not do any great damage. Thus I had been trailed all the way from Strassbourg to Dornbirn in order for them to catch my contacts as well. But the two youngsters had bungled the job. They had arrested me prematurely and so failed to meet Peter. They were very angry and disappointed but I must grant them they were polite and never touched me or even raised their voices. Comparing their watches, they waited hopefully for ten minutes and then stood up to formally charge me with my crimes.

The older one spoke again. "We have sufficient proof of your identity. Your refusal to admit it is therefore futile. The penalty for the crimes you have committed or attempted is death. You will be shot at dawn." Once more I tried to demand a trial but was silenced. Hands tied behind my back, I was returned to the coal cellar for the few hours that remained before the break of dawn.

For a short time I leaned against the wall trying to ease my hands where the rope cut into my wrists. Then Peter came in again and said the Gestapo had left the building. He untied my hands, helped me out of my coat, spread it on the floor and advised me to get some sleep. "Don't worry, Daniella," he said. "You'll be all right. I promise to do all I can to get you out of this fix." Again he left. It was kind of him to attempt to ease my mind but I did not see what he could do for me. He was a police officer and, as such, powerless against the Gestapo. Above all, he was an important link in the Resistance and could not afford to risk his position for a lost cause. I did not really care. Very tired now, I felt, oddly enough, a tremendous relief. At last I had reached the end of a long, lonely trail; no longer would I have to keep running; no longer had I to strain every nerve to keep on the alert, to make quick decisions, to keep awake when all I wanted was to sleep. Now others would have to do the thinking for me. Somebody else would shoulder my responsibilities and I was sure I would not be missed. My child was safe and too young to remember me. With that thought, I curled up in my warm, fluffy coat and, breathing in the faint, sweet scent of perfume my husband had given me on my last birthday, I fell into a deep, dreamless sleep.

In the distance, the rhythmic sound of marching feet was audible. They came closer, marched along the passage outside, turned and stopped. I couldn't open my eyes or move. My limbs felt like lead and my mind was a complete blank. Somebody bent over me and a mournful, disembodied voice said, "Sound asleep. She is only a kid, it's a crying shame. Come and see her."

Another voice from the door answered impatiently, "Don't get emotional again, Willy. The sooner you realize you are here to do a job, the sooner we might make a soldier out of you. Hurry up now and get her out of here!"

The man who had spoken first shook me gently and I opened my eyes reluctantly to look up at him. I saw a boy in uniform, hair cut very short, his face flushed. His childish blue eyes seemed panic-stricken. When he spoke again, his voice was barely more than a hoarse whisper, "Get up and come along."

After the bright, unshaded electric light in the coal cellar, the passage outside seemed very dark and I stumbled over my own feet, still very tired and completely numb. The young soldier put his hand under my arm and steered me along. The other soldier preceded us, opened a door and, between them, they led me out of the building. A closed van was waiting and they hoisted me up, got into the van behind me and closed its doors.

I don't know whether we covered a long or a short distance. Sitting on the floor of the vehicle, I dozed off again until it came to a standstill. Lifted out, I found myself close to a wall at the end of what looked like a playing field. The ground was covered in deep snow. It was impossible to find out where I was. It was dawn and the first faint rays of light could be seen on the horizon and on the steep, snowy incline of high mountains.

The two Gestapo men were at my side again. A short distance away, ten soldiers with rifles lined up.

"Take your clothes off," commanded one of the Gestapo. Everything seemed very unreal and I shivered. I will never forget that morning of February 4th, 1943. It was bitterly cold. The soldiers had mufflers around their necks and snow helmets. Their noses were blue with frost.

"Get cracking, woman," the man shouted. "We haven't got all day."

I took off my coat, sweater and skirt and was allowed to keep on my pants and brassiere. I no longer noticed the cold and felt no emotion. I was a disinterested observer in a numb body.

"Stand against the wall," somebody commanded and, like a mechanical toy, I stood against the wall.

"Have you anything to say?" I shook my head and even that was difficult. My spine was stiff.

"You will be granted a last wish. What is it? Make it snappy."

"I would like to write to my mother, please."

"Oh no, you won't. Think of something more sensible."

"May I have a cigarette?" I don't know what made me say that. I had never smoked in my life and never had any desire to do so.

The Gestapo man handed me a cigarette, lit it for me and I inhaled slowly and clumsily, coughed and tried again, thinking of nothing except how ridiculous the soldiers looked with their blue noses. I recognized the boy who had wakened me in the coal cellar amongst them. Tears were running down his cheeks and he was trying to catch them with his tongue, pulling the silliest faces. That was all that struck me at the time. I thought neither of my family nor my home, nor the past; I just stood there in my pants, watching everything around me and smoking my cigarette. Then, something happened.

There was a commotion at the other end of the field. Somebody came running and stumbling across the snowy expanse, waving his arms and shouting something. Everybody was looking in his direction and not a soul took the slightest notice of me. I think I could have run off behind their backs, but I tried to move and was too stiff and frozen to even lift my feet. Anyway, how far could I have gone in my state of undress?

The man came closer, still gesticulating wildly, and at last I could hear him. "Stop it, stop it, you fools!" he yelled. "Is she alive? Stop it at once!" It was Peter. He gave one glance in my direction and ran across to the Gestapo. They were near enough for me to overhear what was said. Peter told them that HQ Gestapo Berlin had just been on the telephone and demanded I be sent back to them for further questioning. He told them the boss was furious about this bungled job of theirs and he had said on the phone he would soon get that little chit to talk.

Peter turned to me and said gruffly, "What are you standing there for? Get your clothes on and be quick about it. I am now responsible for your safe conduct to Berlin and I'll make sure you don't die of pneumonia before your interview." He turned away and waited till I was ready to follow him. The two Gestapo men stood rooted to the ground. They had nothing to say when I crept back into the same van that had brought me to the field, this time in the company of Peter, my secret friend.

At the station he handed me over to one of his men,

and once more I found myself locked in the coal cellar. Till then I had not realized how very cold I had been. In this hot place my hands and feet began to itch unbearably and I moved as far away as possible from the gate leading to the boiler room. I took my coat off and rolled up the sleeves of my sweater but that seemed to make little difference to my discomfort. Somebody came in and brought a tray with hot coffee and a few rolls, a basin with water, soap and towel. I had a wash and gulped down the coffee and rolls. It had not dawned on me till then how terribly hungry I was, having had nothing to eat for over 24 hours. The man who had brought the tray returned and, at my request, produced a needle and thread. I sat down on the floor to sew up the lining of my coat, the hem of my skirt and the collar of my sweater.

Vaguely, I wondered what would happen next but I felt on top of the world again, warm, relaxed, fed, and very much alive, ready to cope with anything. Soon, yet another police officer fetched me again and said he was to take me to the station to catch a train to Ludwigshafen, a little place by the Bodensee. I faintly remembered passing through it as a child on my family's travels to Switzerland. Naively, I thought I might be put on this train unguarded and wondered which would be the best place to get out and try another escape route. However, at the railway station Peter was waiting with two guards. They put me straight onto the train. A whole carriage had been requisitioned and a guard posted on either exit. Peter pushed me into one of the compartments near the centre, pointed to a seat and posted himself outside the door, locking it carefully.

About 20 minutes later the train moved slowly out of the station, and shortly afterwards Peter came in and sat down opposite me. He looked at me for a moment and then said quietly, "You are a remarkable girl, Daniella. Were you not frightened at all this morning or are you that good an actress?"

He told me the Gestapo Berlin had not phoned him but that he had taken it upon himself to contact HQ on my behalf. He managed to get hold of the Gestapo chief and informed him of my capture. He had added that no documents or proof whatsoever had been found on me to indicate I was the person the Gestapo was looking for. I might or might not know a lot but the officers attached to his station were too inexperienced to find that out. It was then Peter was ordered to arrange for my transport back to Berlin for further interrogation and that was that. He thought the two idiots who had caught me were not likely to find out who phoned whom. He was now going to hand me over to the prison warder in Ludwigshafen whom he knew as an honest, decent man who had no sympathy for the Nazis. That man would see to it that I was detained in transit prisons for as long as possible, probably until the end of the war if the Nazis were not thrown out before then. Peter was apparently a great optimist.

"The rest I have to leave to your pretty face, courage and ingenuity, Daniella. Good luck to you." He got up and looked down at me. He was well over six feet tall, his handsome sunburnt face wrinkled with sadness and worry."Take care of yourself. I'll turn the world upside down to find you when all this is over." He took my hand and kissed it with an unexpected passionate tenderness, turned his back on me and went out into the passage, his head bowed.

He never spoke to me again and I have never seen him since. After the end of the war I heard the rumor that he resigned from the police force shortly after our encounter. Some people who knew him from the Resistance said he had died in a concentration camp, others that he had joined the army and was killed in North Africa; yet another version was that he had volunteered for the

Russian front and was taken prisoner there. I will never know the truth now.

Chapter 4

Handed over, as promised, to the prison warder in Ludwigshafen, I heard the warder assure Peter that he would keep me as long as was humanly possible. I was then locked in a tiny cell containing an iron bedstead, a straw mattress and nothing else. It was the first prison I had ever seen and it seemed pretty grim, but at least it was clean. Not until much later did I realize just how well off I had been there.

For a couple of weeks nobody came near me. In the mornings some gruel and a piece of bread were pushed through an opening in the door; at lunch time there were potatoes, cabbage, or beans swimming in greasy water, and at night some bread, syrup or beetroot jam and a jug of brown liquid, sometimes termed coffee, sometimes tea. There was a bell, however, and on demand the warder came shuffling along and took me to the toilet where I could have a wash in a tiny basin. Once a week, a small wash tub with hot water was carried into my cell and I had a bath. That was most enjoyable until I noticed an eye looking through the peephole. So much for the warder's decency. Apart from washing and eating, there was nothing to do. No books or writing material were allowed and the solitude and silence nearly drove me mad. My mind kept revolving round the mistakes I had made. All that steps I should have taken to prevent walking straight into this trap were suddenly as clear as daylight.

Then I began to worry about my mother, my husband, and more than anything else, my child. For months I had only thought of her during the odd quiet moments and then only with the reassuring belief she was safe, probably sound asleep in a comfortable little cot in a warm, peaceful farmhouse. There were nine children in the family she had been sent to and she would have plenty of playmates and fun, I told myself. The farmer was well off and his wife loved children and had plenty of help. My child would be better fed and cared for than she had been for a long time.

But as day followed day, the memory of my last weeks with Reha became more and more unbearable and again and again the picture of that last night when I had not even had time to kiss her goodbye came back to me. Everything I had done for my child seemed inadequate and heartless. Surely, there must have been another way out of that mousetrap. Had we just thought about it earlier, I could surely have found a hiding place for both of us instead of sending her to strangers. How long was this nightmare going to last? Would I ever find her again? What if Margaret were killed in the bombing? She was the only one who knew the address in East Prussia. I had never taught Reha her real name. Although she was two and a half years old and talked like a child twice her age, she only knew her many pet names so she could not give herself away. Thus, in the prison, I tortured myself until I could no longer sleep or eat at all, I must have looked a wreck too, for, when the Gestapo turned up one day to verify the warder's statement that I was physically unfit for transport to Berlin, they just took one look at me, nodded and left again.

Then one day the door of my prison cell opened and two girls walked in whom I had known very well in Berlin. They, too, had been caught and arrested somewhere near the Swiss border. They were a bit more fortunate in that they were not married, had no family ties, and had not been connected with any Resistance organization. They were very young, 17 years old, light-hearted, and seemed to treat jail and everything else as a huge joke, an experience not to be missed. However, they were quite convinced they would soon tire of it all and would then walk out and try some other route to Switzerland. If they were not cracking jokes, they were always hatching some crazy plans for escape. So, the next three weeks were bearable, even though the cell was so small that two of us had to crouch on the bed if one wanted to pass to the door. We had to share the one bed at night, and, as we were all big girls, that was not easy. Eventually, we slept in shifts and that worked out quite well. The two youngsters managed to distract me from my unhappy memories. I felt I had to mother these two children for, although I was only 20 years old, I felt like 100. But they did make me laugh, at times so much the warder admonished us to keep quiet, at least until the Gestapo left the building in the evening.

The girls had been with me for nearly two weeks when one night, at some ungodly hour, the warder called me out. I followed him with apprehension and was taken to a washroom. He locked me in, switched on the light from the outside and there, in front of me, stood my husband. It was like a bad dream that must surely end soon. But it was no dream. He was there all right. He, too, had made a beeline for the Swiss frontier, the only chance of escape at that time, had duly been arrested and was on his way back to Berlin. His clothes were in a pitiable state but he looked strong, healthy and sunburnt. He seemed older and more mature than I remembered him. Seeing me alive, his spirits rose tremendously and all his exuberance bubbled up. For the next few minutes we laughed and cried in each other's arms and for a few more days the prison warder locked us together for an hour every night after the Gestapo had gone. We continued where we had left off, making plans for the future. And then he was gone again—in a transport, handcuffed to a criminal. We saw him leave when we were in the yard walking round and round for exercise, a privilege recently granted to us for "good behavior."

He saw me too as he, with eight or nine other men, escorted by armed guards, marched through the prison compound. Handcuffed, he could not wave but nodded his head in my direction, a boyish grin on his face as he tried to keep his unruly, brown hair from falling into his eyes. As he passed, he called over to me, "See you soon, my darling. Keep your chin up." For that, he got a rifle butt in his ribs that would have sent him sprawling had the man to whom he was handcuffed not given a jerk and pulled him up.

I was kept in the prison of Ludwigshafen for six weeks, first because of my alleged ill health, later because scarlet fever had broken out in one of the transit prisons and a quarantine was ordered for all prisoners en route to Berlin. But eventually the ban was lifted and the warder could no longer find any valid excuses for holding me back without risking his job and security. One day, therefore, about the middle of March, the two girls and I were taken to the station and put on a prison train consisting of many carriages, with no windows other than small barred light shafts in the roof.

We passed in transit through eleven different jails before we reached Berlin. Generally, we spent the night in one of them, were put on the train the next morning, travelled an hour or two, were again unloaded and taken to the next prison. There was nothing remarkable about this journey. Some prisons were dirty and we had to sleep on damp stone floors in the company of prostitutes and petty thieves; there were rats and the warders were indifferent to our misery. Other prisons were spotlessly clean with blue and white or red and white gingham sheets and bed covers. In these places there would be a bath or a hot shower, better food, and generally some sympathy for our unusual position. There we would be kept apart from criminals.

I remember Heidelberg particularly because it was such a lovely day when we were unloaded from the smelly train. The sky was a perfect blue and the air was warm and heavy with the scent of spring. Through the barred windows of a police van we could see the bright yellow jasmin bushes, gardens with crocuses and daffodils and the first primroses. The longing to be free was so great it seemed to burst my heart. There was no hope of escape—we were so heavily guarded—and I just buried my face in the perfume still clinging to my coat and no longer looked out through the window at the glorious spring.

As we travelled further north towards Berlin, we left spring behind and hope for some miracle, the end of the war, or the overthrow of the Nazis, dwindled.

Chapter 5

Now here I was in Berlin again, free, leaning against a tree outside the prison gates, deeply inhaling fresh air and basking in the sunshine. It seemed a miracle had happened. At last I tore myself away and started to walk. I was not quite certain which way to go to get to my mother at the hospital, but what did it matter as long as I could keep walking? I had all the time in the world. I went round the first corner, light-headed and somewhat unsteady as though I had just got up for the first time after a long illness. Then suddenly, I heard echoing footsteps behind me. Before I could turn around, two men got hold of my arms and one put his hand over my mouth to prevent me calling for help. They pushed me into a taxi. Looking around frantically, I realized the street was deserted and there was no point in protesting. One of the men gave the driver the address of Gestapo HQ, an address well known and dreaded by everyone in Berlin. The cab moved off, silently and speedily.

On arrival, the men took me to a large reception room, full of people, men and women. They all seemed to be waiting for something. Some stood around in groups talking loudly and nervously about football, school, or a dance. Others tried to walk about but never got very far before more people blocked their way. Some stood dejectedly against a wall, their faces white and strained, and if anybody tried to talk to them they turned their heads away or looked right through the speaker and didn't answer. They seemed more dead than alive and only when a name was called did they jump into galvanized attention, just to slump down again if they were not wanted.

In the taxi I had slowly accepted the idea of finding myself a prisoner once more and got over the initial terrible shock. At first I wondered if I might not have escaped had I walked in the opposite direction or had I not waited and day-dreamed so long, but common sense told me the trap had been laid anyway. The reason for this cat and mouse game was obviously to keep prison staff and the general populace ignorant of our fate. It was designed to make them believe young people who had committed some blunder were taken into custody and then sent home to their parents.

By the time I reached Gestapo headquarters, I could, once more, laugh at my own stupidity at having been taken in so easily. In spite of rumors about the activities and cruelty of Gestapo officers, I was not afraid, certain they would know all there was to know about me. They would also know that I was a very unimportant link in the Resistance, small fry, who could not give any information even if I had wanted to do so. In any case, from the time I was recaptured after my short-lived freedom, I no longer gave any thought to either past or future but lived solely in the present, paying attention only to my immediate surroundings. I still believe this detached concentration kept me alive through all that was to follow.

I did not have to wait long. A young man, well dressed in civilian clothes opened the door and smoothing down his wavy blond hair, called my name. When I stepped forward, he said politely with a very cultured voice, "Do you mind coming to my office for a minute? We just want to ask you a few questions relevant to our reports. Do go ahead, please." The door of the waiting room closed behind me and the young man preceded me up the stairs. He took me to an office with two desks. Another man was seated behind one dictating something to a very glamorous secretary. He got up when I entered and I noticed he was tall, dark and handsome, although not at all the fair, blue-eyed German ideal. His face seemed friendly and honest. He dismissed the secretary and told her he would call her when he had seen this young lady—meaning me.

He walked round his desk, offered me a chair and asked me, ingratiatingly, to sit down. He sat on the edge of his desk and lit a cigarette after offering me one. The second young man who had brought me upstairs, sat down behind another desk and, apparently, looked through its drawers for some papers.

The secretary had left the door slightly ajar and I could hear her high heels clicking down the stairs. There were the usual noises one hears in any office building—a telephone ringing somewhere, somebody calling for a clerk to get some files, typewriters being hammered on steadily and, downstairs, a low humming of voices, probably coming from the reception room. The fair-haired man got up and closed the door and the world from me.

"Where is your child?" the tall dark man barked. He was towering over me now, his face revealing his true self. It was terribly frightening, this fearful, undisguised, savage brutality. I jumped up from my chair without thinking, but in retrospect it was probably to escape a veritable villain.

He did not give me time to think. His right fist struck me under the chin and I fell back on the chair. His companion, almost immediately, jerked the chair from under me, and as my reactions were too slow after the blow, I found myself on the floor. The fair-haired fellow grinned like a schoolboy playing tricks on somebody, but there was no change in the other man's face.

"Get up you bitch! Get up before I help you," he said in a quiet but all the more dangerous voice. I got up and squared my shoulders, prepared for another blow.

"Where is your child?" Again, I did not have time to think but there was no need to think. Something deep inside me felt elated, singing triumphantly: My child is safe! They can do what they like, but my child at least is safe. I had expected questions about my relations and activities with the Resistance, queries about its members and organization, but this I had not anticipated.

My mother and I had agreed, should we ever be interrogated, we would say we had sent the child to Italy, but Italy was no longer a safe place and any such statement could easily be investigated and disproved by the Gestapo. On the spur of the moment, I said that friends had taken her to Switzerland. Another blow of that hairy, big fist, a kick in my abdomen, another against my knees, a right-handed hook that seemed to close my eyes, another on my nose and mouth and I felt the blood running down my chin.

Flattened against a wall, I stood up straight. Between blows the same monotonous question: "Where is your child?" But no time to answer, more blows, more kicks. The room was reeling around me, faster and faster. No more pain, everything numb. Suddenly a pause, silence, no more beating. My ears were singing, my head was swimming and I heard my own voice, unnaturally loud:

"You cowards, you terrible, beastly, murderous cowards! Aren't you ashamed. How do you face your mothers or your sisters or your wives if you can treat a woman like this, a woman who has done nothing but try to save her child?"

A sudden, exploding pain in my head behind my eyes and then peace, nothing, darkness and silence, a blissful eternity; something fiercely burning, tearing, hitting my back galvanized me out of unconsciousness. I screamed, "Oh, Mother, help!" The younger of the men got hold of the whip my tormentor was swinging over me.

"Not now," he was saying, "too many people in the building. We'll get her back at night and she can scream the house down."

"All right," they pulled me up by my hair. "You'll tell the truth when we tear the skin off your back strip by strip, gorgeous."

The dark man caressed the knotted leather thongs with an evil grin. "We'll get your mother now. She might not be so tough a nut to crack. Good of you to call for her. I nearly forgot her. She won't be much use to you by the time we have finished with her but she might be useful to us. . . . Take her through the back door, you don't want to frighten newcomers with that apparition."

Through the back door into another police van I went, and after a short drive, found myself in the courtyard of a very familiar building. Previously my domestic science school, it had now been turned into a reception camp for prisoners due to be deported. After the heavy school gate closed behind me, I was met by friendly, clamoring voices in one of the corridors. Somebody eased me gently onto a mattress on the floor and soft hands put a cold, wet cloth on my aching forehead and swollen eyes. A girl pulled my clothes off and bandaged my lacerated back.

Everything seemed unreal and far away, but I was very conscious of having called for my mother when that beast was beating me. I did not keep my mouth shut.

I had reminded him of her existence, betrayed her, and soon she would go through the same ordeal because of my weakness and cowardice.

There were voices, young voices, all around me, trying to talk to me, asking questions, talking to each other. My eyes were too swollen to open, my lips were cracked and I could not talk. But my brain was active now, going over the last few hours, visualizing my mother under the same circumstances, abusing myself, hating myself.

I don't know how long I had been lying there. Somebody poured a drink of cold water through my teeth and placed new cold cloths on my head. A girl was talking quietly. She said I would be all right now, and the transport to the East was due to leave in two days. They were all from camps where young people had been trained in agriculture and forestry, preparing to emigrate to Palestine. She told me she would look after me till I felt better and that we all, young and strong as we were, would survive hard labor in the East. After the war was over, we would go to Palestine together.

She was very kind and I felt her dry the tears that kept running uncontrollably down my face. I wondered whether she would still be so concerned if she knew I had called out for my mother under the first impact of torture.

It seemed like a dream when I heard my mother's voice calling me, but there she was, kissing me and stroking my swollen face. A jab of a needle in my arm and a little later I felt fine, sat up, and carefully opened one eye. My mother was there, unharmed, looking well and still in her nurse's uniform.

She had been arrested at the hospital, had been taken to the Gestapo headquarters, saw the same two men and was asked immediately where her grandchild was. She, too, remembered our agreement but, thinking quickly along the same lines I had, replied that friends had taken the child to Switzerland. The two men thanked her for the information and she was sent to the deportation centre without being troubled further.

We were together, alternately laughing and crying. She told me my husband had been taken to the Jewish hospital two days ago with scarlet fever. She had seen him; he was in high spirits despite his illness and sent me his love. He was going to be well looked after by my mother's best friend, a senior sister on the isolation ward. He would be kept there for another month or two. Anything might happen to help him during that time.

Just a few days before her arrest, my mother had managed to buy a Danish passport for herself and my child, but a Jewish boy had been picked up with a similar passport and his own identity card. After that, any Danish identification was automatically suspect and it would not have been safe to make use of it. In any case, there had been no time to bring my daughter back from East Prussia and my mother's dream of disappearing quietly to Denmark came to nothing. We decided therefore to stick to our story if we were asked about the child again.

The days passed quickly and the transport was postponed. I got better, the swelling all over my body subsided, turned black and blue and then faded. Only shock remained to a certain extent. The days were not too bad. We became very friendly with the boys and girls from the agricultural camps. They were all strong and optimistic and morale was high. Only at nightfall did I become terrified, afraid to sleep, and shaking with fear of being called back to the Gestapo. It happened eventually. I must have been white with terror and lack of sleep. The short trip was agony. Yet when I got to the HQ, there was only an elderly man who was in charge of prisoners at the Jewish hospital, the same man who had warned my mother of the deportation of young women and children.

He spent hours with me, patiently explaining that I could save my mother if I told him where I had hidden my child. He said I would be allowed to take my daughter with me to the East. He guaranteed we would not be separated and that my mother could stay and work at the hospital unmolested. He promised me my mother's life and safety but, he said, "You have to answer to God for what is going to happen to her if you don't answer my question. Her life is in your hands."

Had I not known the experience of a few days earlier,
I might have weakened, but as it was I knew our days were
probably numbered. We were in the hands of the Gestapo,
but my child was not and she had a reasonable chance of
being saved. The officer then told me that my tormentors
had advocated the deportation of my mother alone and that
I be kept until they could make me talk. However, he was
their senior and had decided we would be deported
together for the sake of my mother of whom he thought the
world. He said he would kill me with his own hands if he
thought he could thus save my mother's life but, unfor-
tunately, he was not a free agent. It was not in his power to
save her, but, he repeated, it was in mine. He informed me
we would be deported on April 20th, an extra large transport of young, strong Jews in honor of the Fuehrer's
birthday. After that, Germany could be considered free of
Jews; the rabble of old and infirm people left behind did
not count. They too would soon be eliminated.

And so the day of deportation dawned. It was still
dark when we were herded into trucks which took us out of
Berlin to a freight train depot. We were unloaded and then
started a seemingly endless roll call. Five hundred boys
and five hundred girls were there from all the training
camps in Germany: strong, healthy, good-looking youths.
Truly a proud sacrifice to the Fuehrer! When the roll call
was nearly over, another two trucks arrived. Out of them
the SS pushed and kicked old men and women, mostly on
sticks and crutches, the remnants of two homes for old
people. At the last, there were 20 young women with small
children. The latter arrivals were not called or counted but
loaded straight onto one of the wagons of a long, long cattle train. An SS man came over to us and said to my
mother, who was still in the uniform in which she had been
arrested, "You better get in with the old people. They
might need a nurse."

I tried to follow her but was pushed back into the group of young girls. However, just as my mother was getting into the wagon with the old people, the Gestapo man from the hospital turned up, took her by the arm and led her back to me. To the SS guard he said, "She will be more use to those fit to work." Once more he turned to me and almost pleaded, "Save your mother! Talk. Tell me where your child is and I'll take your mother back to the hospital in my own car." My mother only shook her head and he turned away and left us.

We were soon loaded into the cattle trucks, 50 boys and 50 girls in each wagon. We sat down on the straw-covered floor, the doors were closed, barred on the outside and locked. In almost complete darkness, a boy started to play a mouth organ and another an harmonica, first an old Jewish marching song and then the tune that was to become the Israeli national anthem. As the train began to move, we all sang, joined by many young voices in other parts of the train. Rolling east, we sang. It was a sweet and powerful song. We knew we would be free again and show the world that youth would never be defeated, but at what price this future freedom? At what price? We could not have answered that question and we did not ask it then.

Chapter 6

On and on rolled the train; through the day, through the night. When the small toilet bucket in a corner we had screened with straw was near overflowing, we banged against the wooden planks of the cattle truck. To no avail. A giant of a boy battered the wood until it splintered and he managed to break a hole just big enough to empty the bucket. We could thus keep the carriage reasonably clean and aired. In other wagons they were less fortunate and many of the old people suffocated in their own dirt.

Gradually the boys and girls fell asleep. In their youthful health they barely stirred. Nestling against my mother and covered with my warm coat, I too felt drowsy and very tired when I sensed rather than heard the young man next to me shake and sob quietly. He had been so cheerful all day. He resembled a sunburnt Greek god, his profile sharply edged against the gloom. His beautiful voice had carried us from song to song. But now he was crying. I moved away gently from my sleeping mother and put my hand on his curly black head. He started and whispered an apology.

"Tell me why you are crying?" I asked quietly. "Have you left someone behind?"

"That's just it, Daniella, I haven't. For the past three years I have subjected myself to an iron discipline. I was not going to touch a girl until we were settled in Palestine. No girl was going to be tied to me until I could offer her freedom for our children and happiness. And now it is too late. If I had only once kissed a girl. . . . Tell me, what gives you the courage to smile and joke as if you hadn't a care in the world? You have left a husband and child behind and while I felt like crying all day, your voice was so genuinely jubilant. Do you have no regrets because you knew love and fulfillment? Or are you so sure you'll survive and find your family again?"

There was no answer to his questions. I could not have explained even to myself why I felt so free and reckless under such hopeless conditions. Perhaps it was because I thought my child safe. Perhaps, because I had been too young for all that heavy responsibility and was now, regardless of outcome, unable to do more. Yet, somehow, I felt responsible even for the despair of this young stranger and had to make an effort to share my peace of mind. So I gently turned his head until his face, wet with tears, touched mine. I kissed his salty tears away and felt his fresh breath on my face. It was no sacrifice to kiss his soft young lips. I imagined it was my husband I was holding and felt him relax like a little boy after a nightmare.

"You darling, darling," he whispered, and his husky voice seemed already far away in the land of dreams. He slept peacefully all night, his curly head on my arm.

He is dead now and I don't even know his name. But does it matter? Dead, too, are all the other 499 strong young men of our transport. I wonder how many of them had never kissed a girl, had never lived at all?

The train slowed down and stopped abruptly. Dogs barked, men shouted commands, iron bars screeched and sliding doors creaked. It seemed an eternity till our wagon was opened. A few boys and girls who had been jammed against the door fell out and the ones next to them were roughly pulled out by SS men. Within seconds we were lined up in blinding sunlight. There was no station, no platform, no houses, no trees; only yellow mud trampled hard by our predecessors. There were a few patches of tough grass and nettles of the most poisonous green I had ever seen. Somebody whispered we were in Poland.

My mother stood beside me and held my hand. We noticed suddenly that all men had been taken from our ranks and were standing with the men from the rest of the train some distance away. At the other side of our group were the old people.

An SS guard barked a command: "Stand to attention! The doctor is going to examine you all."

A tall, dark man in the uniform of an SS officer appeared and went slowly through the lines of prisoners. Not until much later did we learn that this young SS officer in his elegantly tailored uniform and shining boots was Dr. Joseph Mengele, chief doctor of Auschwitz-Birkenau concentration camp. He was present at the arrival of every transport from every country in Europe and was in charge of the "selection."

Born into a wealthy family—his father was an industrialist in a small Bavarian town and the farm machine factory is still owned and run by the Mengeles—Joseph was a privileged and gifted child. As a young man, he first studied philosophy and later medicine. Always involved in right-wing politics, he was fascinated by Hitler's oratory and joined the Nazi Storm Troopers in October, 1933. He soon adopted the Nazi doctrine of Aryan superiority and got involved in research to find proof that defects of race are inherited in racial genetic make-up.

While he amassed honors in peaceful research, he was not keen to pull his weight when the war broke out. Transferred then from a post as health inspector for the SS to the Viking Division, composed of Scandinavian volunteers, and later to the SS infantry on the Eastern front, he was afraid to fight in Russia. Due to his SS connections and patronage, he managed to get himself transferred to Auschwitz where he was soon appointed Chief Medical Officer. From then on he was entitled to kill or save hundreds of thousands of men, women and children.

Now, at our first encounter, he looked at each girl in turn and said, "Worker, to the left." He stopped in front of a middle-aged woman who, like my mother, held her daughter's hand. "You need an easier life, mother. To the right."

She didn't understand, did not let go of her daughter's hand and pleaded, "I'm only forty. I'm strong and I can work. Leave me with my child!"

"Forty is too old," the doctor said and beckoned to a guard. The tough SS man pushed her into the group of old people who tottered under the impact. The doctor passed on to the crying girl: "Worker, to the left." And on: "Worker, to the left."

Another fifteen or twenty joined the workers. He stopped again and fixed his piercing eyes on an undersized, young girl with a beautiful thin face, huge, dark, luminous eyes, and a slight hump-back. "Too weak, needs good, long rest. To the right." She went over to the old people.

He had nearly reached us. I whispered desperately, "Mummy, say you are 35!" She looked younger. The SS doctor had reached my mother. He looked at me. "Is this your daughter?"

"Yes," said my mother.

"How old are you?"

I kicked my mother lightly. "I am 41," she said.

He hesitated a moment. "Senior nursing sister?"

"Yes," said my mother.

"Worker, to the left." He went on and on.

Nearly all the young girls from the agricultural camps joined us. All mothers with young children went with the old people. The husband of one of these women had an artificial leg. He went with the old people and young mothers. His wife was sent back to the workers. He lifted his small child and waved with his free hand to his wife. The child laughed and waved too.

Then we were told to start marching. I can't remember how long we walked through the desolate country. The most striking feature was the poisonous green grass and a few stunted trees. We passed innumerable watchtowers, all manned by armed guards pointing their machine guns in our direction. All around us were armed SS guards and their huge German Shepherd dogs yapping round our feet.

At last we stopped and were counted in front of an open gate in a barbed wire enclosure, studded with watchtowers. Over the entrance, in large letters, were the words, *Arbeit Macht Frei*—Work Liberates. We passed through the gate and through a neat, clean square of painted wooden barracks, surrounded by beds of struggling, undernourished flowers, and were herded into a huge barrack with a mud floor. The wooden doors closed behind us and, again, we were in semi-darkness.

An SS guard went past and told us to roll up our sleeves and to hand in identity cards and passports. When he took mine, I asked when we were getting them back. With a nasty grin he answered, "You don't need passports where you are going."

There was no doubt about the meaning of his words and there, in the dark, was born my stubborn determination to survive our enemies and torturers. Slowly, we were pushed forward towards a fire in an open grate. Behind it sat a man with a long needle in his hand. He turned the needle in the flame until it was red-hot and then stuck it into the forearm of his victim. Again into the fire and back into sizzling skin. Surprisingly, there was no sound, save a quick intake of breath or a short gasp. Nobody spoke and the silence, darkness, the fire in the grate, and the smell of burning skin reminded me of stories I had read of human sacrifices to ancient gods.

The first girls came past us to take their place at the end of the queue again, and, nursing their sore arms, showed us what the red-hot needle had accomplished: a big, long number across the centre of the forearm and a triangle underneath: a tattoo. My turn came. An SS man immediately twisted my arm back, almost dislocating my shoulder in the process. I became number 51459. Much later I learned what these figures meant: 51,000 prisoners had come here before us and almost 45,000 had already died to make room for us. That number did not include the old people, mothers with children, the weak and the sick who were never tattooed at all. In the meantime, we were branded like cattle.

On either side of us SS guards lined up. "Get ready for delousing! Clothes off!" their officer shouted. Nobody moved. The first SS men advanced menacingly on the frightened girls in the front row and, grabbing their dresses, tore off their clothes until the girls stood naked and shivering with fear and shame.

"I can't face this," my mother whispered. "I'd rather die. Let's get out of it." She pulled a small bottle and a hypodermic syringe from her pocket but before she could get the needle into the bottle an SS man hit her across the wrist with his revolver. The syringe and bottle dropped onto the hard ground and broke. To make doubly sure, the man ground his heel on the splintered glass.

My mother's clothes were torn off, but not before she had withdrawn her hairpins, allowing her long black hair to cover her like a silky coat down to her thighs. I stripped my dress off before the men could get their hands on me and felt no shame. We had to parade through the double line of leering guards to a row of chairs and there the "delousing" began.

Our hair was cut off and our heads shaved so close to

the skin that our skulls were grazed. We then had to lift our arms and the hair under the arm pits was shaved. Last and worst indignity of all, we were hoisted on to the chairs and had to submit to the shaving of pubic hair while the guards looked on with sneers and obscene remarks. This went on till late at night.

We were dazed with cold, shock and hunger. The last sandwiches we had been given by the nurses of the Jewish hospital in Berlin had been shared out and eaten before we were unloaded. Two naked bulbs illuminated our sorry spectacle. I did not recognize any of the girls with shaved heads. I could not find my mother and called out for her, frightened suddenly, like a child alone in the dark. She was right beside me. I had not recognized even her brown, burning eyes in the white face. She looked like death and I turned quickly away to find some consolation in the round, healthy limbs, proud young breasts and the stubborn, con-temptuous faces of the girls of my own age.

At last we were given some clothes. Each girl received a pair of pants, many without elastic, a tattered, faded summer frock, mostly too large and too long. Some even got wooden sandals. Rags though they were, it was something to cover our nakedness and to hide us from the untiring, leering inspection of our guards.

At the end of the barrack, double doors opened and we were marched through a flood-lit camp past many wooden huts. Between the huts we could see electric barbed wire fences and watch-towers. Outside the fence, flood-lit too, were brick buildings with tall chimneys smoking furiously, often emitting flames that seemed to shoot up to the starry sky. An evil, sickly-sweet smell combined with acrid fumes assailed us from their direction and stung our eyes.

"These are our most productive factories," grinned one of the guards. "Working day and night shifts, and if they don't purify the air here, they certainly clean up the rest of the Fatherland."

Except for the guards talking and laughing, the deadly silence around us was complete. Outside one of the long buildings we were stopped and counted once more. Then, admitted in twos through the entrance, we were met just inside the door by a young woman in a lovely dressing gown, high-heeled slippers, beautifully curled black hair and carefully made-up face. She had a notebook and pencil in her hands and a stick under her arm. With an amazingly deep voice that belied her feminine appearance, she raved at us to get in quickly and to keep the cold out.

We moved along a narrow passage, almost dark, on either side of which were double-tiered bunks of bricks, some covered with a little straw, most of them bare. We moved a bit further along and heard the doors close behind us and then all hell broke loose. Inhuman voices screeched, whined and shouted from the bunks around us. Shaved skulls and death-like skeletons shot out and peered at us from all sides. Fleshless claws stretched out and touched our clothes, faces, and arms and an unbearable stench of unwashed, diseased bodies enveloped us. An Inferno! For the rest of my life I have had this vision of hell indelibly imprinted on my mind.

Rapidly we were pushed into vacant bunks, ten of us in each tier where there was barely room for three. My arms round my mother's shivering shoulders, I stretched out as far as was possible on the cold bricks. Ten human sardines lying on our sides, unable to move or turn around, we spent the rest of the night in fitful slumber, interrupted again and again by screams born of nightmares, by hollow coughing along the passage, by cold and by hunger.

Chapter 7

Midway between seconds and eternity we were roused by the deep voice of the house Capo in charge of us: "Roll call! Get up you filthy B's! Roll call!" She went past the bunks, holding a handkerchief over her nose with one hand and, with the other, hitting immobile backs with her stick. Most of the poor skeletons were galvanized into movement but there were a few who did not respond. Beaten and shoved, they fell off their bunks in untidy heaps, received a last kick from the high-heeled slipper and lay still. A few had escaped the roll call, cold, hunger and degradation. They were quite dead. They were left where they had fallen; the living scrambled over their bodies, out of the hut into a cold, dark April morning just before dawn.

For two hours we stood in lines, clapping our hands and each others' backs in an effort to get warm. At last, an SS woman, accompanied by two guards and two dogs, came along and counted our ranks. The woman was very young and fair, her face expressionless. She asked the house Capo for a report. The Capo, or Blockova, as she was commonly known, reported the number of dead with a curious expression of satisfaction as one might expect on reporting a great achievement. The SS woman nodded, marked a list and called out tattoo numbers. I had to look at my arm before I realized I had been called.

The roll call over, we were allowed back into the hut, received a chunk of bread each and a chipped enamel bowl containing a lukewarm, black liquid—"tea." The bread was to be the ration for the day but we were so hungry, we wolfed it down there and then. My mother and I shared one bowl of the dark brew and kept the other under our bunk to wash our hands after the old inmates had been marched off to work. So far, we had seen no water.

We sat on our bunks wondering what was going to happen next and tried to understand what we had so far seen. We speculated about the factories, the dead who had been removed, the SS woman, the big, solid crystals in the bread. Many of us were desperate to get to a toilet but didn't know where to go. We were not permitted, under threat of being shot, to leave our hut until the Blockova came back from the gate where she was signing out the workers in her charge. When she did return, she herded us to the lavatories, a long building with frames for doors, but no doors and no roof. The conveniences consisted of rough wooden planks laid over seemingly bottomless pits where rows of women perched precariously like sparrows on telephone wires.

Tripping delicately through mud and puddles, the Blockova next pointed at the washrooms, another long hut with concrete floors and rows of taps. There she left us with the admonition that we were to be back in our barracks in ten minutes "or else." We found to our dismay that in the whole washroom only one tap was working and it was guarded by a huge Polish woman.

The girls had politely made room for my mother to have a wash first, but when she tried to get to the tap, the woman pushed her back forcefully so that she landed in my arms. In Polish, accompanied by violent gestures, the Pole gave us to understand that this was her domain. Nobody used this tap unless they paid first. One bread ration, margarine or sausage was the privilege of a wash, half a ration for a drink. I tried to reason with her. After all, she was a prisoner like us. However, when she advanced on me, tight fists ready to strike, and when my mother tried timidly to pull me away, all self-control left

me and I hit the woman across her broad face with the flat
of my hand. She stumbled and slipped on the wet floor
and, getting gingerly to her feet, removed herself cowed.

We all had a wash. There was no soap and no towels.
We got back into our rags soaking wet but refreshed and I
had learned my first lesson: unless you answered violence
with violence, you were doomed.

Back in our barrack, we saw the Blockova through
the open door of her room preening in front of a mirror,
intent on making up her face and pinning up her shiny,
black curls. As she paid no attention to us, I decided to
have a look around the camp and left my mother with the
other girls.

The camp seemed deserted. A warm sun burned the
caked mud and, except for the guards on the watch-towers,
there was not a soul around, no sound of birds or any other
living creature. Absolute silence. Even the factories and
their tall, red chimneys were dead. No smoke.

At last, turning a corner, I saw an old woman sitting
with her back to the wall of a hut, warming her thin
shoulders and claw-like hands in the sun. Her head was
shaved, her wrinkled little face seemed almost blind but
she could see for she motioned me to sit down. I sat down
beside her and introduced myself. She said her name was
Ruth and told me she knew what transport I had arrived
with. She smiled a little. "We know everything here.
Nobody tells us, but we know. We even know when our
friends are going to die just by looking in their eyes." I felt
uncomfortable and she guessed it immediately. "Don't
worry, you'll live. You have the strength and the
willpower. In two or three weeks' time you may be a
skeleton, but you are a fighter. I can tell you will not lie
down and die willingly. Look at me. You wouldn't think I
was 19 years old, would you? But it's true, my 19th birthday was two days ago."

I felt myself flush and turned my face away. An "old woman" indeed. What had they done to her here?

"I'm sorry you feel embarrassed. Don't. I am finished with this rotten world. There's no future for me. My mother, father and little sister were killed and there is nothing for me to look forward to. Don't mind me though. You are so young!" That from a little old woman of nineteen. In spite of myself, tears were welling up, hot and stinging in my eyes.

"I don't want to live, but may I help you and give you some hints that may come in useful?" Ruth had been in Birkenau, the death camp, for three months. On arrival, she had been separated from her parents and little sister and grouped with the workers. Only one woman over 40, a tall and beautiful woman, had been allowed to enter the camp with them. A few days ago, that woman had run from a dog the guard had set on her and was torn to shreds. There was not enough left to bury. Her name was Paula Raphael and, if I ever met her son, would I tell him that she was dead but that she had spoken of him, his young wife and child.

Paula, my lovely mother-in-law! I swallowed hard, but said nothing. I wanted to know all there was to know.

Lesson No. 1: Don't ever run away if an SS dog is after you. Stand still, even if he has his fangs in you and he'll let go.

The "factories" were gas chambers where whole transports of old people and mothers with children were given a piece of soap and a towel and then driven into huge rooms with innumerable shower heads in the ceiling. When the doors closed, gas instead of water poured in through the sprays. After a few minutes, the bodies were dropped through trap doors into the crematorium and burned. Night after night the chimneys belched forth their black clouds of smoke. A special commando of prisoners served in the gas chambers, removing valuables, rings, gold teeth and the like from the dead, and after a term of service, were gassed themselves and replaced by a new lot of prisoners. Once the commando was chosen, it never came into contact with the rest of the camp again.

The Capos and Blockovas were prisoners like ourselves but after years of concentration camp life, they had learned, if they survived, to be tough, cruel and thoughtless. Often they were just a shade more cruel than their masters. Thus, they were a privileged class. Most of them were Slovaks, some were German, non-Jewish prisoners who wore a green triangle on their dress, indicating they were criminals. Others were professional prostitutes who had refused to do war work in factories outside. They had been sent to the camp to be "rehabilitated." However, here they played with human lives and at the same time carried on their profession with SS guards and passing German soldiers and, of course, developed all the perversities under the sun.

If the Blockova kept back half your food ration, you had no redress. She was quite entitled to kill you. She could torture you or put your name and number on the list of those no longer able to work and so detail you for the gas chambers.

Although officially you were entitled to nothing but the rags you were given on entering the camp, nobody turned a hair if you were clever enough to "organize" decent clothes as long as they were marked with your number, red triangle (for political prisoners) and a large red cross painted on your back. In fact, if, by stealing, you managed to look clean and well dressed, you were sure to get better and easier work. Ruth did not know how to go about getting new clothes. But she knew that Capos all had friends among the prisoners who worked in the stores where clothes from newly arrived transports were sorted and dispatched to Germany's bombed cities. You could change your rations for clothes on the camp's black market but Ruth had always been too hungry to save as much as a crumb. Now that she was no longer hungry, she also had no desire for a pretty dress. "Does it matter in a mass burial how you are dressed? If your clothes are worth looking at, they are stripped before your body is cold anyway."

Ruth told me that the SS woman who had taken our first roll call this morning was Irma Grese who was only 17 years old. She had been recruited by her lover, an SS officer of unusual cruelty and perversity. Irma was getting a thorough training in the art of torture and killing.

I also learned that the crystals in the bread were a chemical which, given in quantity, completely suppressed any normal sex instincts and menstruation in women, and made prisoners dull and easier to handle.

Ruth closed her eyes and her head sunk forward. I felt she had, for my benefit, spent her last energy talking. I got up and apologized for tiring her out. "I better get back to my hut now, but I'll be back tomorrow with some bread for you," I said optimistically.

She smiled a sweet, tired smile. "You have to eat all the bread you can get merely to exist. Thank you just the same, but I won't be here tomorrow."

"Where are you going?" I asked foolishly. Ruth grinned happily but did not reply. Instead she said in a voice so low I had to bend down to hear her at all:

"Goodbye, good luck, and my love to your mother. She must be a wonderful woman. You are so lucky to have her around to keep you alive." Not until much later did I realize I had not mentioned my mother. But there was much I had to learn before I knew from experience all the things one understands when one is about to die.

As I turned the corner to our barrack, I saw the girls were lined up and a big, fat SS officer was strutting up and

down in front of them. The Blockova jumped at me like a
cat pouncing on a mouse, grabbed me by the shoulders and
propelled me forward. She was much smaller than I, but it
did not occur to me to resist. Just as she was going to
shove me into the last row, the SS man called to her to
bring me to him. He looked me up and down and rumbled,
"Are you one of this transport?"

"Yes."

"Hm, from Berlin?"

"Yes."

"Is that so? I'm from Berlin myself. Have a soft spot
for girlies from our great capital. What were you doing?
Playing truant already?"

"No, I just walked around to have a look at the camp."

"Adventurous type. Liked what you saw?"

"Of course not. It's the most evil place I ever dreamed
could exist!"

"Well, at least you are honest. Tell you what," he said
jovially, "made up my mind to give the girls from Berlin a
chance. You are a good-looking healthy lot. I'll make you
a special working commando, an example to the rest of the
camp, with uniforms—say, striped dresses, aprons, headscarves, blue or red—and double rations. How would you
like to be a Capo?" he asked me.

I said I'd hate it. "From what I have seen and heard of
Capos and Blockovas so far, they are a despicable lot."
Our Blockova turned as red as a turkey's neck.

The officer gave a deep, rumbling laugh. "That's
enough of your cheek. One day in camp and no respect
yet? I'll teach you. You are the Capo of the Berlin Commando and you better do well. Keep fit, clean and healthy
and you won't regret it. By Jove, if you don't make these
girls work, you'll have to answer for what's coming to
you. Off with you now! Get deloused, new clothes, double
rations and tomorrow morning you'll collect vegetables

for the camp kitchen. That's your first assignment and then we'll see again." He turned to the Blockova. "If you don't treat these girls well, you'll go digging trenches. I'll ask if they have any complaints. So you better behave. They are under my protection." He explained he was the labor leader and repeated unnecessarily that he, too, came from Berlin. He flicked his whip and disappeared. I have forgotten his name now, but he was as good as his word.

We were led to the sauna. Only nothing here worked as, I presume, it works in Finland. The steam was so hot it scalded our skins. Fortunately, this ordeal was of such short duration no serious damage was done. The water after the steam was icy and, as we had each been given a piece of soap, we made the most of it and covered our bodies with a rich, if peculiar smelling, lather. That done, we discovered the water had ceased to run. Probably a little practical joke of the sauna Capo. We had no towels and our old rags had been removed. All we could do was to scrape the soap off as best we could and leave the rest to dry and cake on our skins. At last, prisoners brought in heaps of grey, blue-striped dresses of a heavy, warm material, blue-checkered headscarves, aprons and a pair of leather sandals for all of us.

Back in our barrack, we were given a bowl of soup, an extra bread ration with a piece of margarine, a spot of beetroot jam, and a piece of sausage. The soup was the most peculiar dish I had ever eaten in my life, but one got used to this conglomeration of potato peelings, greenery, odd pieces of Turkish delight or caramels and even sodden rolls of bank notes swimming in it at times. We felt heaps better, warm now, adequately, even neatly dressed and no longer hungry. For the rest of the day we were left in peace except for another roll call after the return of the workers.

The Blockova was now ingratiatingly friendly and told us of her early days in the camp. She had arrived in

winter before there were any huts. The whole of
Auschwitz and Birkenau were nothing but vast fields of
deep, yellow mud, fenced in by barbed wire. Just before
her arrival it had been a camp for Russian prisoners of war
and she still found innumerable bodies half-buried in the
mud. For days she existed and slept in the open. During
the day, she and others of her transport collected and
buried the dead, decaying bodies. Later they carried
stones, bricks and timber many miles to build our huts.
The barracks were then built in record time by male prisoners, none of whom were now alive. Of her transport
only she and two of her sisters survived. She made no
secret of the fact that they had achieved this by stealing the
clothes and the bread rations of their unfortunate fellow
prisoners who were too weak to fight. I tried to imagine
what she had gone through to find extenuating circumstances for what she had done, but it was impossible.
The sight of her well-fed, well-groomed, self-satisfied face
made me shudder with horror.

Just before dark she distributed horse blankets, one to
every two or three girls. There were a few more bunks
available and we spent a slightly better night than the one
before.

The following morning after roll call, we were
marched off to the gate where a yellow armband with
"CAPO" printed in large, black letters was pinned to my
right sleeve. We were then given baskets and an escort of
four guards with the inevitable German Shepherd dogs at
their heels. After being counted, we left through the gate
with the words "Work Liberates" above it. We were
marched into a fresh, sunny morning, through poisonous
green fields and the illusion of a certain freedom, to collect
"vegetables," that is, nettles for the camp kitchen. There
was no scarcity of nettles in that area. In fact, I have never
known of any other place in the world where there was

such an abundance of nettles growing to man's height. All day we picked nettles, and in no time were covered with irritating, burning blisters all over. It was agony at first but one got used to nettle stings too in time.

The guards did not trouble us. They had been told we were under the special protection of the labor leader. They teased us for a while, calling us the "Berlin Elite" or the "Beauties of the Kurfuerstendamm," but they soon got bored and gave it up when we didn't respond.

In the afternoon we returned to camp, roll call, a wash, and double rations, but before we had to turn in for the night, I took my extra ration and walked round the block to find Ruth. She wasn't where I had met her the previous day and I went into her hut where I was met by a dragon of a Blockova. Just as she was going to turn on me, brandishing a stick, she saw the "CAPO" on my sleeve. So she checked herself and listened to my question. "Ruth, Ruth? Oh, do you mean that useless B that was always sitting in the sun? She kicked the bucket last night. Buried her this morning, good riddance! Had her on my hands far too long. She was always moping about and refused to work from the very beginning. No interest in anything. Well, she'll rot in her grave now for long enough."

I turned on my heels and ran back to our barrack, shaken to the core. But I didn't mention Ruth even to my mother who knew me so well; she understood without my saying a word that I had seen a ghost. Nor could I bring myself to enlighten the others about the "factories" or anything else I had learned. They'd find out soon enough. Just now, they were so happy about the apparent consideration of the SS labor officer and his order to our Blockova—the woman in charge of our barrack—to be friendly "or else," they were laughing and fooling around. I knew that we would not laugh again for a long, long time. A few more hours or days without that dreadful knowledge of realities would therefore not hurt the girls of my transport. So I wiped away the tears surreptitiously and listened to their excited chatter, to somebody aping the labor officer's sonorous voice, "I'm from Berlin myself. Have a soft spot for the girlies from our great capital . . . " and to their uninhibited laughter.

Chapter 8

A few more days passed, one like the other. Sometimes the roll call took hours and, on one occasion, we stood lined up all through the night because somebody had tried to escape and didn't return from outside work. However, no escape was successful in those early days. The prisoner was always tracked down by the dogs or, if she got far or even managed to get beyond the radius of guards and watchtowers, the Polish population invariably handed her over to the SS and Gestapo. The runaways were, at that time, always Jewish prisoners. German inmates were too placid and well-fed to bother, conscientious objectors and Bible students believed in the inevitability of their martyrdom, and gypsies were too frightened. The Polish population could recognize a Jew or Jewess no matter how well disguised, and if they hated the Germans, they hated the Jews more. They were most helpful in the total elimination of their Jewish problem. Thus, sooner or later, the culprit was returned dead or alive, and if the latter, was publicly tortured and hanged.

The whole camp had to look on and SS guards went through our ranks to make sure nobody turned their eyes from this ghastly spectacle. I got into the habit of standing with my eyes staring straight ahead but seeing nothing. My brain refused to take in what I must have seen. The roll call ended when the hanging was over. During this night-long roll call, my mother collapsed. She had not been well for days, was white as a sheet and very weak. There was no medicine unless one went to the camp hospital, but once there, there was little or no chance of surviving. The patient might, on occasion, be treated but even if she recovered, she was generally sent to the gas chambers at the weekly selection from the sick bay. Knowing this, we bullied and threatened the Blockova into concealing my mother in a bunk the next morning and reporting her as essential for cleaning work in the barrack so that she would not have to go out to work.

When we returned that night, she came out for roll call but was too weak to stand up and we carried and held her until the guard had counted us and moved on. Then we lowered her gently on the ground until whistles were blown and we could disperse. During the night she tossed and turned and shivered although we had collected four blankets to cover her. In the morning she was so ill, not even black tea would stay down. She had not been able to eat her rations for the past three days.

I left her with a very heavy heart. Up to this day we had filled our baskets with nettles in no time at all and then sat down in the grass doing nothing, preserving our strength for things to come. Even with double rations we were beginning to get thinner and weaker. Still, in comparison with the other prisoners, we looked fit.

Always good at relaxing and doing nothing, I just could not sit still today and time did not seem to pass. When another Capo with her commando came by and yelled at us to get up and work, it was a relief to put out my tongue and tell her to mind her own business. "Leave my girls alone," I called over at the top of my voice, looking at her group of poor skeletons who could hardly drag one foot in front of the other. "We are not all murderers. My girls are going to be alive when you have to answer for all you have killed."

The Capo shook her fist at me and one of our guards said, "Now you've done it. Can't you count your blessings and keep your trap shut? That one is the most notorious Capo in Birkenau. She'll report you and when you return to camp, you'll lose your armband and I'd be surprised if you are still alive a week from today. We will probably go on extensive exercises, if not the Russian front, for allowing you to be lazy."

I was too worried about my mother to listen and did not care, but, right enough, when we reached the gate in the afternoon, a voice shouted, "Berlin Commando halt! . . . Capo, fall out!" I stepped out and an SS woman tore the armband off my sleeve. To the accompanying guard she said, "No. 51459 gets no rations tonight. Report to her House Capo: no sausage, no margarine, no jam for three days. Half bread ration only and two weeks hard labor. Berlin Commando, march!"

The guard handed me over to our Blockova with his instructions and I slipped past her before she could open her mouth to see my mother. But my mother wasn't there. Her blankets were neatly folded on her bunk and there was no sign of her anywhere. I ran back to the Blockova. "Blockova, where is my mother?" Like the guard earlier, she said, "Now you've done it, you stupid B! Don't you know when you're well off? Your mother is all right, she'll survive you now. She has been chosen to go to the sewing room in SS staff quarters in Auschwitz. They have tiled bathrooms there, single beds, good clothes and plenty of food from the SS kitchen." I did not believe her.

The SS had a well-known trick. From time to time they went through the camp after workers had left to take weak and sick prisoners to "Block 24." That dreaded and notorious barrack was the collection centre for the gas chambers. There the condemned were kept up to two weeks until the required number was complete. Once there, there was no hope of escape. The victims were fully aware of their imminent end and their demented screams haunted our dreams at night.

Most prisoners who were left behind in the camp now

hid under straw mattresses or in the eaves of the roof as soon as SS approached. Therefore, in order to find as many victims as possible with a minimum delay and fuss, SS administration had developed a new system. They produced a list of vacancies at other, better camps, desirable posts in factories or staff quarters, ordered the Blockovas to find prisoners to fill these vacancies and left. Needless to say, there were many volunteers, and when the SS returned half an hour later, their required number was waiting. It took a long time before the truth trickled through and a rumor went round that these appointments did not exist and that all volunteers had ended up in Block 24, and subsequently "gone up the chimney," the expression used by the SS and hardened camp personnel for those gassed and cremated. There was no way of finding out for sure whether my mother had shared their fate. It was no more possible to enter Block 24, a barbed-wire stronghold within the camp, than it was to fly to the moon. The condemned were completely isolated and no word or note ever found its way out. Nothing mattered to me after that. I had brought this fate on my mother. If she was dead, I had helped to kill her!

The girls tried to press some of their rations on me that night, but the mere thought of food choked me. The following day I went out with the hard labor corps. We worked from morning till night carrying rocks and digging trenches until we dropped. Night after night we carried our dead back with us. If twenty went out in the morning, no more than ten returned. The weakest died and the rest were assisted in dying by unmerciful kicks and beatings handed out by brutal guards and Capos. I learned much later that no more than half our number were supposed to return to camp at night, and if not enough died of their own accord, the guards had a last resort. They dropped their caps or drinking bottles some distance from our place of work and sent a number of prisoners off to retrieve them. As soon as the poor wretches had gone a few yards, they were shot down like clay pigeons, or worse, torn to pieces by the dogs. At the gate the guards reported that three, four or five prisoners had tried to escape and had to be killed. I found out too that the guards of these hard labor commandos got a bonus for every dead prisoner they returned to camp, a day added to their annual leave and an extra cigarette ration.

Apart from the odd kick, nobody ever touched me, probably because I was still the strongest of our sorry lot. At night I dropped into my bunk and slept, too tired to even collect my half bread ration. Often in the morning, I found crumbs of sausage and margarine almost devoured by rats, remains of rations my friends had left beside me. In that short period of hard labor, I had grown indifferent to rats, comfort or discomfort. I functioned like an automaton whose clockwork was slowly running down.

My punishment ended on the morning of May 19th, 1943 after exactly two weeks. At the gate I was called out and the labor leader asked me if I had learned my lesson. There was no need to answer. He returned me personally to our Blockova with the instructions that I was to have a hot bath, delousing, clean clothes, and double rations once again. I was to have the day off and rejoin my group the next morning. We were to be incorporated into an "elite commando," the "white caps," so called because of their white headscarves. They were detailed to sort out clothes and belongings of all newly arrived transports.

So far, this commando had consisted of the prettiest girls from Eastern Europe who had been in the camp a long time. They held all the key positions and regarded prisoners of all other nationalities with contempt. They were physically much tougher than most prisoners from western countries. They had become used to a hard climate and harder conditions and they had survived many ordeals. They had, by now, lost almost all scruples and conscience: we newcomers had not. For that they despised us and exploited our vulnerability.

The steam bath and delousing was a great ordeal this time. I was very weak, and more than once nearly fainted. The Sauna Capo again turned off the water before I got a chance to wash off the soap and I no longer saw any humor in her pranks. The palms of my hands and my arms were grazed and raw from carrying rocks and the strong carbolic soap burned and irritated my skin. For the third time since my arrival barely a month ago, my hair was shaved and my scalp felt sore.

When I walked out into the blinding sunlight, I experienced for the first time a sensation which was to repeat itself many a time. All feeling of despair and exhaustion left me suddenly. I felt weightless, no longer earthbound and had the sensation I could fly if I wanted to. At the same time, an urgency I did not yet understand drove me to rush back to our barrack. It was nearly midday. The sun was high up in the sky; the camp was quiet and deserted. There was no sound.

The Blockova was waiting for me with double rations. She inspected my clean dress, apron and white headscarf and said, "You look a bit of a scarecrow, don't you? You'd better start eating again if you want to keep up with the White Caps." With unexpected friendliness she added, "Look here, you just have to be smart if you want to survive. That dress is too long. I'll pin it up for you and give you some cotton. You can shorten it before the others get back."

I wondered vaguely where she managed to get such treasures like pins, needles and thread, but I was restless and she kept telling me to stop fidgeting. I felt there was something I had to do, and suddenly I knew. Almost like a third person, a surprised observer, I heard myself say, "Leave the dress just now, please. I must get to the sauna to see the new transport from Berlin." I did not tell the Blockova that my husband and child were with that transport, but I knew.

She looked at me with a mixture of contempt and fear. "Have you taken leave of your senses? There is no new transport today. I would be the first to know. Blockovas are always given a few hours' warning to make room for new arrivals." I said nothing and spent the rest of the afternoon turning up the hem of my dress with shaking hands.

My rations remained untouched; I could not eat. Innumerable times I felt a compulsion to jump up and run to the sauna but all that afternoon I fought that impulse. As the day wore on, my certainty grew but the Blockova was watching me in such a way, I was beginning to doubt my sanity.

The girls of my transport came back from work and, immediately surrounding me, shook my hands and kissed me. They had not changed. Still full of hope and vitality, they told me I would soon be strong once more. They would see to that, and we would go to Palestine soon. Then they buzzed off to get their food rations and only my two bunkmates stayed with me, their arms round my shoulders. When we were alone I told them of the new transport and added that my husband and child had arrived too. Like the Blockova, they did not believe me and Susan said gently, "As far as I know, there is no transport today but even if there were, Daniella, your husband might be with it but not your child. Haven't you told us your baby is safe? You know that better than we do. Come on, pet, eat your sausage and calm down. Two weeks' hard labor was no joke but it is over now. Please, for your own sake and for the sake of your mother, you must eat. You know your mother would have died happily if she knew you were going to live. You owe it to her."

I made an effort but still could not eat and the whistles for roll call stopped all further attempts. As soon as roll call was over and the girls were filing back into barracks, I slipped away and ran all the way to the sauna. The doors were locked and there was no sound. I waited and waited. Susan came looking for me. She put her arm round me and told me to come back with her to our bunk. It was getting dark, she said, and it was time to go to sleep. I hardly listened, and eventually she shook her head sadly and went back to her younger sister, alone.

It was quite dark and the camp was floodlit when the sauna doors opened and the new transport came out. Among the first were the two girls I had met in prison in Ludwigshafen. Shaved and branded, their spirits were, nevertheless, as high as ever. When they recognized me, they fell round my neck and cried, "Are you still here, Dannie? Do you know the layout of this dump yet? We'll have to get out of here smartish like. We'll make plans tomorrow. If we three can't escape, nobody can."

They suddenly sobered and Hannie looked round and asked, "Where is Frau Unger? She said she was your teacher at Domestic Sciences in Berlin and you were her favourite pupil. Have you not seen her yet? She took your child from your husband before the men and women were separated and promised to bring her straight to you. She felt we women could look after the children better than these wretched men. Frau Unger had your daughter and her little stepson by their hands. An SS man demeaned himself to carry her luggage. Then we lost sight of her somehow, but ours was such a big transport. I think she must have arrived here with the first batch of women and children."

The last words I heard as if through a thick fog. I

turned and ran, ran and ran: To the electric wire, to peace, oblivion, death. Oh God, the gas chambers are belching smoke and I am enveloped by thick, black clouds of it. The acrid stench of burning flesh is choking me. Let me get out of it, please, just the last stretch! But there was no end to this long road, no kind God to take me by the hand and lead me. I did not make it. The world reeled and vanished in absolute darkness. I fell and knew no more.

Chapter 9

The awakening was slow and painful. Susan and her sister Lorna were bending over me, pouring hot tea down my throat. I swallowed greedily and couldn't remember what had happened to me. The Blockova came along and fed me with small pieces of chocolate, undreamed-of luxury. Somebody said, "Get up, lazy bones. You've slept through and missed roll call already. Time to move out with the White Caps. We are going to work in Canada."

The Blockova anticipated my incredulous query and shrugged her shoulders. "Why is it named Canada? Probably because of the barrack's multi-racial contents or perhaps workers have such soft living conditions there." She drove the girls out in her usual rough manner, although she had given up hitting us and even seemed to have some affection for the prisoners in her care. When I passed her, she pulled me back into her room, a cubbyhole she had all to herself, and said, "Listen, Daniella, I have sent word to the men's camp to have your husband taken to the barracks where you are going to work. This is your first day there, so be careful. If you have the Dutch SS woman as a guard, you'll be all right and can spend some time with your man. She'll turn a blind eye. But should the guard be changed today for some reason, you'll have to give it a miss and try meeting him tomorrow. My sister will keep you right. She is in the Canada commando too. Another bit of advice: Organize some decent clothes for yourself and your husband. My sister will give you number tapes and red paint to fix his number and the red cross on the back of the jacket. The chances are he will get a better kind of job if he is well dressed. I'll explain the system some other time. Get out now or you'll be late."

Only when she mentioned my husband did the events of the previous night come back to me; but something had changed. My heart was hard and heavy like the rocks I had carried but I did not want to die any more. Suffering would come later. Now, I moved out with the others like a machine. At the gate we were told by the labor leader that he would deal personally with any one of us who looked or spoke to any of the men we might see around the barracks we were to work in. He made it clear that an ordinary death was too good for a prisoner who had any dealings with the other sex.

A tall, fair SS woman strode alongside us and we moved off through another gate into the men's camp of Birkenau. The road into that camp was lined with male Capos waving and leering at us. It was surprising to see that nobody seemed to take the slightest notice of the warning we had just been given. The old core of the White Caps gaily waved to the men who threw packets of cigarettes, sugar and chocolates which the girls in front of us caught and quite openly stuffed into their apron bibs and dresses. The SS woman laughed and joked with the male prisoners, calling them affectionately "lazy Bs" and "filthy pigs" and graciously accepted a large box of cigarettes and a bottle of French perfume from the tallest prisoner. He was a German criminal with an armband inscribed "Lager-Aeltester" (Camp Senior) on his sleeve. She received a few more packages which she handed over to some of us to carry for her as those in front of us were already loaded with presents of their own. We realized that the privileged male prisoners paid her well for keeping her eyes and mouth shut. Once she had her dues, she hastened to drive us into the huge barracks, loaded from end to end with mountains of clothes, shoes and suitcases.

The Capo explained we were to sort out men's and

women's clothing. Once separated, we had to make parcels of different items—shirts, trousers, socks, underwear, ties, dresses, blouses, skirts, stockings, etc. We were to look for valuables, money, jewelry, cigarettes concealed in the clothes and hand them over to the SS woman. In a low aside, she murmured, her lips barely moving, "If you know what's good for you, you give them to me."

So, our work began. All these things, stacked to the barrack roof, were to be bundled, packed and readied for dispatch to Germany by the afternoon. If the target was not reached, there were threats of punishment ranging from overtime and reduced rations to transfer to outside or even hard labor. All that did not worry me. I was completely indifferent, but remembering the words of our Blockova, I immediately set out to find suitable clothes for my husband.

There was one corner at the far end of the barrack that was almost completely cut off from view by heaped bundles of clothes and stacked suitcases. The Capo soon disappeared behind them. "There is a small door there," one of the girls who had worked here before said, following my glance. "That's where our boyfriends come in. As long as the SS woman and the Capo get their share of the loot, they don't molest us. The men bring us all kinds of food from their camp kitchen that ordinary prisoners never see and we give them clothes in exchange."

In no time at all, the bundles were separated and I had no difficulties finding the right size of shoes, socks, underwear, shirt and sweater for Freddy. There just remained a suit and that was more difficult. He was tall and most of the pants and jackets seemed too short in the legs or sleeves. And then I found them: his own sports jacket and flannels. I recognized the handkerchief with his initials first. These clothes were all from his transport. These were the belongings of all the men and women who had entered the gates of Birkenau yesterday and were freezing in their miserable prison rags while their good, warm suits and dresses were being sent back to Germany's Nazis for their "Winterhilfe" (Winter Aid).

As soon as Freddy's outfit was complete, I found our Blockova's sister. She showed me where to paint the red cross all over the back of the jacket and where to sew on the number tape with a red triangle. The number itself would have to be filled in with indelible ink once I got it from my husband. She also gave me a packet of cigarettes, matches and a bar of chocolate to put in his pockets. Turning away to hide her tears, she said gruffly, "I haven't done much good to anybody so far, but you are the first woman lucky enough to have her husband alive in this camp. Do you know what that means? Men are even weaker and more helpless than we are and if you can't pull him through being in this commando, may you rot in hell! I know you are a Jaecke (a name of contempt given to German prisoners by those from Eastern Europe) and probably as stupid, stiff-necked and scrupulous as the rest of your crowd, but I can tell you now: If you don't learn to steal, cheat, lie; if you can't walk over dead bodies physically and metaphorically and learn that damned quickly, your next port of call is the gas chambers. Now get on with your work till you are called."

She folded my bundle of clothes neatly and took them behind the wall of clothes and suitcases at the far end. She told me where to find them later and went on with her own work. We all continued sorting and bundling quickly and automatically. One or the other of the old girls kept vanishing at the far end to have a smoke, and I discovered for the first time the calming effect it had on my nerves and I smoked until it made me feel faint and dizzy. At noon, prisoners from the men's kitchen brought huge containers with steaming food and everybody got a good helping of meat, potatoes, cabbage and gravy. For the first time since my mother had vanished, I ate properly.

The Dutch SS woman had so far taken little notice of us. If she wasn't laughing and flirting with the men, she was stretched out on a heap of blankets, smoking and reading a book or combing her long, golden hair. Shortly after the noon meal, however, she called me, the first and only guard to use my name. Usually, we were just numbers. Inspecting me with some curiosity, she said, "You have a very good-looking husband. Better do something about his appalling clothes. I haven't seen him or you or anything else though, understand? Scram!" She pushed me off in the direction of the far end.

He was waiting for me behind the protective wall of clothing. In spite of his shaven head, he still looked the most handsome boy I had ever seen. He still seemed so well and strong that his pitiful rags went almost unnoticed, but something about him struck me forcefully: he stood rooted to the ground and there was such terror in his eyes that I had the impression he did not see me at all. I ran to him and threw my arms around him and could feel his heart beating wildly through his thin, torn shirt. Before his hands touched me limply, he looked round him like a hunted animal and did not speak. I assured him it was all right for him to talk to me here, and at last he looked up and stared at me.

"Oh, my darling, what a nightmare this is! I can't bear it. You look so thin and ill. Are you all right? . . . Two men of my transport hanged themselves last night. One pushed the house Capo by mistake in the general upheaval and the swine beat him to pulp. Oh God!" He put his hands up to his face and seemed to forget my presence. I pulled them down gently and shook him.

"Freddy, pull yourself together. The first night is the worst, believe me. Once you are working you will find it more bearable. You just have to believe me. I've been here a month now. Listen, I have found your own clothes and painted the cross on. Put them on quickly and I'll fill in your number. Once you are decently dressed you'll be all right and get a better job in your camp. Don't ask me why; I don't understand it myself yet. They take all your own things, yet nobody asks where you suddenly manage to get new clothes from. You'll just have to accept the fact that no normal values are accepted here." I pushed the suit at him and begged him to hurry up but he did not move.

After an interminable silence he said, "I can't do it Dannie. You don't know our house Capo. He is a murderer, the devil incarnate. He'd kill me if I turned up in these clothes. Thank you darling, but I can't change into them." I begged and bullied him, but he was adamant and so frightened I finally gave up. I had failed him too. The words of our Blockova's sister kept haunting me. Henceforth my soul would "rot in hell." Had I known then what I learned later, I would have bought his Capo. I should have sent for him first. I should have given him a suit better than the one I had for my husband and assured him of new clothes as he required them. Freddy would then have been all right and unmolested and, what is more, would have been well fed and given work within the camp.

Once my husband had refused the clothes and I had given up the struggle, he seemed to feel better and cheered up a bit. He suddenly asked, "How did you find Reha? Hasn't she grown? Was she happy to see you and is your mother looking after her?" He did not know anything yet.

I hid my face on his shoulder so my eyes would not let him guess at the truth. "Yes, darling, she is all right. My mother is looking after her and both are much better off than you and I. How did she get into your transport?"

He looked surprised. "Did Mrs. Unger not tell you? Margaret's brother in East Prussia got scared because the child had no identity papers and his party leader kept badgering him about that. So in the end, after another phone call from him, Margaret had no option but to collect her again. She brought Reha back to Berlin and left her on the doorsteps of a Catholic orphanage. The nuns kept her there and looked after her well. But the Gestapo took photographs of all foundlings and took them round hospitals and other institutions to find out if anything was known about their parents.

"A woman detective in plain clothes turned up at the Jewish hospital where I was with Scarlet Fever. She left the pictures on the police desk and sat down in a corner. One of the younger nurses came in later to see the matron about something, took one look at the photos and cried, "What a lovely child! Isn't that the granddaughter of Sister Elizabeth? She is her absolute image." Of course, the detective jumped up and soon found out who Sister Elizabeth was and that I was her son-in-law. She brought Reha to my ward. I denied desperately ever having seen the child and put my finger on my mouth when nobody was looking my way, but Reha came running to me. She climbed up on my bed and shouted with all the joy of a lost three-year-old, 'Daddy, my Daddy!' The game was up then and I took her in my arms. She was so happy that I reproached myself bitterly for ever having gone along with that crazy plan of yours to hide her. Her place is with you and even this hell is better for her as long as she can be with you and your mother. Nobody can be cruel to a beautiful child like ours."

I shook him wildly, "Haven't you finished yet, you fool? Find out where you are first and what your child has come to." I quickly checked myself and apologized for my lack of control. The future was bleak enough for him and he would find out all too soon. Why could I not keep my mouth shut and leave him with his illusions and an incentive to live for a little longer?

He did not appear unduly upset by my outburst though, and said tenderly and humbly, "I was a beast, darling, complaining of hardships when you have already had such a time of it. It can't last forever though. Just keep your chin up and we'll soon be together again and I will look after my family." Just then the SS woman poked her head round the corner and told him he'd "better buzz off." He kissed me and left. All I had managed to force on him was the bar of chocolate, cigarettes and matches. I went back to join the other girls with the knowledge that I had failed them all, my mother, my husband, my child. I had believed myself to be strong and intelligent when all I had been was vain, arrogant, immature and cowardly. I thought my heart would break with the pain of the immense vacuum that was my future.

At our return to the gate that night, our guard made a great show of examining us for loot. We all had to step out one by one and raise our arms. She slid her hands down our hips, fronts and backs and found nothing, although some of the girls were so obviously bulging that I trembled in case somebody noticed it. In the end she put her hand in one girl's apron pocket and pulled out a packet of cigarettes. With the labor leader and all other SS officials and guards watching, she slapped the girl's face, called her a "filthy B" and worse, and announced the girl was to go on half-rations for two weeks. That, in our commando, was a farce. Through the men and the clothes she could smuggle into our camp and exchange for food, she would not have starved had she been given no rations at all.

I did not see my husband again for a long time, but he managed to send me a note nearly every day and I sent him cigarettes, extra bread rations, margarine, sugar and onions, sometimes even chocolate for which I had exchanged clothes. He still would not hear of taking a good suit but he would accept clean underwear and socks. He was working on rail repairs, and although the work was hard with long hours, his notes were cheerful and optimistic. The days were warm now and with the extra rations he kept up his strength. Our days went by with regular monotony, but that did not worry us unduly.

The chemical in the bread was achieving its objective. It not only prevented menstruation, but also dulled our senses to such an extent that we no longer felt much initiative or desire for action. Even fear and pain were dulled and blunted. There remained just a dumb instinct to survive.

New transports arrived day in, day out. If we left the barracks empty in the afternoon, they were stacked full again with fresh loads in the morning. By the quality, texture and colors of the women's dresses more than from labels, we could tell where the transports had originated. There were well-made dresses of good, solid material from Holland; smart and beautifully tailored French models; lovely embroidered blouses and fur coats from Slovakia and Hungary; light, flimsy flower-printed frocks from Greece; and headscarves, aprons and shawls in glaring colors from Gypsy transports. Hundreds of men and women of all these nationalities entered the camps every day. How many more had perished in the gas chambers?

The chimneys were smoking day and night. It was no longer possible to see the sun in daytime or the stars at night. A thick blanket of smoke enveloped the camp and the horrible smell stung our eyes and nostrils even if the wind carried the smoke away from us. But the days were bearable. Engaged in this futile, depressing work I was at least surrounded by my friends who tried with infinite patience, love and tenderness to instill some hope and purpose into my almost demented mind. There was the incentive of keeping my husband alive. The nights, however, were terrible. I could not sleep. The barking of dogs and the SS shouting and often shooting off rifles round the gas chambers were enough to drive even the sanest person crazy. The smoky stuffiness of overcrowded barracks was unbearable.

Susan and I, when her younger sister slept, sometimes crept out in the middle of the night to try to get some fresh air but there was no fresh air anywhere. If eventually I fell into exhausted, fitful sleep, I always had the same dream: I saw Mrs. Unger coming towards me, carrying Reha and leading a little boy by the hand. She smiled and called out to me. I ran towards my child who stretched out her arms, but as soon as I came near enough to almost touch her, the road became a fast-moving conveyor belt and carried them away from me to a brick building with a huge iron door and a tall chimney. They vanished through the door and when I caught up with them at last, the iron door closed in my face. I heard my child's faint cry, "Mummy" as the door banged shut and then silence and no sound other than my fists battering and my feet kicking against the door. My friends who shared a bunk with me always woke me up then for I was hitting and kicking them cruelly.

Such was my state of mind when, one evening after roll call, the Blockova asked me if I would like a change of scenery. A new working group, the "shoe commando," was being formed. If I wanted her to put my name on the list, I would be loading shoes into wagons outside the staff headquarters in Auschwitz and could, maybe, see my mother. At the same time, I could do her a favor and contact her sister who was Capo of the SS laundry there. The last time she had heard from her, over six months ago, her sister had promised in a note to arrange a transfer to the staff quarters. Since then she had heard nothing. I did not believe my mother was alive but I felt this was my only chance to find out what had happened to her. When my friends promised to look after my husband for me and carry messages between us, I volunteered.

Chapter 10

The SS women's staff quarters was a large, square building standing isolated in the barren landscape near the small town of Auschwitz, about twenty minutes' march from Birkenau. There were a few trees around the house, but at the back, railway tracks ran immediately below the iron-barred basement windows.

The first day I arrived there, the whole length of the building was cut off from view by an immensely long freight train. On our side of it were mountains of shoes ready for loading into the gaping doors of the wagons. The shoes must have been collected from many, many transports of prisoners.

A guard ordered me to get inside the first of the trucks and stack shoes the other girls threw in. All day we loaded and by evening the mountains seemed barely diminished. Yet we had filled six trucks to their roofs. A few times I tried to slip behind the train to get a look at the basement windows but the guards and their dogs were on alert. One step away from the allotted place of work and the nearest dog let out a deep, low growl, lifting his massive head and baring his teeth; the SS man relaxed his grip on the leash and released his rifle's safety catch. By evening we had not even a glimpse of a single prisoner inside the staff quarters. For three days we worked and loaded the train and at last it was full and moved off slowly to make room for the next. There was our chance. The barred basement windows were full of excited faces calling out to us, asking for relatives in Birkenau, shouting out names I had never heard. My mother was not there. Our guards relaxed and looked the other way when we edged nearer to the windows. At last I got close enough to a girl to ask for my mother, making two or three attempts before my voice was audible, fearful of the answer.

"Sister Elizabeth? Yes, of course, she is here. She has just been summoned to give an SS woman a massage. She had hoped to get news of you through her. Why didn't you answer her notes?" the girl asked indignantly. "Don't you know your mother was wearing herself to a shadow thinking something had happened to you?"

I had never received her notes. Just before the guards whistled for us to line up for the march back to Birkenau, I managed to say, "Give her my love. Tell her I am quite well and I'll be back tomorrow and every day now till I can see her." Then I remembered to ask for the Blockova's sister. She was at the window and told me she was still trying to get her sister over to the staff quarters and hoped, with my mother's help, to get her soon.

For the first time I felt alive again. My mother was really alive and well and even seemed to be in a position to do something for prisoners in Birkenau. How or what I did not yet understand, but I would soon see her and find out. The march back to camp was nothing; there was hope. After roll call, I gave the Blockova her sister's message and got double meat and fat rations as a reward and ate them. My friends were jubilant when they heard about my mother. It was almost as though she was the mother of them all and the whole of our barracks celebrated. We sat on our bunks, even the Blockova, and pooled our resources. There was even a whole cigarette for each of us.

The next day I saw her. The guards were a more decent lot and didn't appear to notice if we slipped between the trucks to the basement windows. My mother was pale like the others for want of fresh air and sunshine, but well fed and clean and her lovely black hair was growing again. The privileged prisoners of the staff quarters did not have their heads shaved.

My mother told me she had volunteered that day so long ago, convinced she would end up in the gas chambers, but she was determined I should not see her die a slow and painful death. All other prisoners had gone into hiding and she was the only one that could be found. There had been a long argument between the SS that day about whether they should take her, the poor, sick apparition that she was. In the end they decided they must have somebody quickly to mend silk stockings. For once, the "job offer" was not a hoax. Now tears were rolling down her cheeks, but she was so happy to see me, words failed her.

In the staff quarters' basement were housed not only prisoners who worked in the SS laundry and sewing room but also female prisoners employed in the so-called "political department" of Auschwitz. There the SS kept records of all people who entered the various camps in that area. Furthermore, with typical Prussian thoroughness, they listed the names of those who entered the gas chambers too. The women working in that department were sworn to secrecy and any leak of information was sufficient to justify their deaths. However, when they heard I was coming to see my mother they had prepared her. So she knew that my husband was in Birkenau and knew, or guessed, what had happened to our child. As always, she was stronger than I and talked to me about Reha, about Freddy and our extreme youth and our chances for the future. I could see her heart was breaking, yet I greedily absorbed all the love and hope she held out to me, and as usual, could give little in return.

One morning as we were marching out, my husband entered the women's camp. I had a note from him telling me he had been given carpenter's work and that his next job was to roof a block of latrines in our camp. In passing he threw me a kiss and his enchanting smile and whistled a few bars of several songs. Knowing their lyrics, I understood something was happening in Italy and Russia. We didn't get any news, but occasionally something leaked through by word of mouth from prisoners picked up in France, Holland or other occupied countries.

Freddy was thin but cheerful, as straight as a rod and taller than any of his fellow prisoners. When I had heard he was coming to our camp, I had arranged with the Blockova to keep me back for house duties soon so I could meet him. But I didn't want to stay the first day because I knew my mother would get a terrible fright if I suddenly did not turn up with the shoe commando. I hoped to explain to her why she would not see me for a day or two and I did get a chance to talk to her that day.

"Be very careful, darling," she warned me. "Don't risk your life or his unnecessarily when you talk to him." She ended up saying: "You don't know, sweetheart, what terrible consequences your meeting could have if you don't watch out. I won't be happy again until I see you back here."

The words and tone of her voice so reminded me of that far away day in Denmark after she discovered me on top of a sand dune in the arms of a young Danish student. The memory of that first, very harmless kiss made me momentarily forget where I was and I broke into helpless laughter. "You shouldn't let him kiss you," she had said on that beautiful summer holiday when I was twelve years old. "You don't know the terrible consequences your secret meetings might have. You are much too young. Why you might even have a baby." She had never been able to bring herself to talk to me about sex, but even then I knew it was pretty safe and certainly wonderful to be kissed. However, I did not get a chance to explain what I was laughing about and later on I forgot. She must have thought I was out of my mind.

My heart was pounding from the time I woke up at dawn. The roll call seemed endless. Today I was going to see my husband, speak to him, bury my head on his shoulder and, if only for a moment perhaps, kiss him again. The longing to be held, to feel small and protected, grew unbearably. Our Blockova had given me to understand there would be no difficulty in getting him alone. The men's guards were usually too busy with German prostitutes during working hours to worry about the prisoners. They knew that escape from within the camp was a physical impossibility. Once more I was going to persuade Freddy to wear good clothes. My friends would get them for him and we knew the ropes by now. Surely now he had more experience of camp life, he would accept them and better his chances for survival.

At last the roll call came to an end and the working groups moved slowly out of the gate. Susan had supplied me with a new headscarf and apron; others had given me chocolate and cigarettes for my husband. To pass the time until the men arrived, I helped the regular house staff straighten blankets and sweep the barracks until the Blockova came in to say the men had started work. I dashed off in the direction of the new blocks toward the sound of sawing and hammering. Creeping round the last corner, I found their guards were nowhere to be seen and I could go right up to the men. The new buildings kept me from being seen from the watch towers. About ten prisoners were working there but my husband was not among them. An awful fear gripped me, and the longing to see him became an unbearable necessity. I recognized the boy who had walked beside him when they passed me yesterday and I went up to him. "Where is Freddy Raphael?"

He glanced at me casually and said, "He was gassed last night, poor chap. We had a big selection yesterday and everybody who was underweight or looked ill, or otherwise didn't come up to standard was taken to the gas chambers. Freddy had a sore throat and his voice became very hoarse towards roll call time. When the SS walked through our ranks and asked him his number, he croaked in reply. That finished him. They killed over a thousand of our men during the night."

The ground seemed to rock under my feet and I instinctively covered my face with my hands to ward off the blow. The boy looked at me and asked gently, "I say, are you a relation of his?" I could not answer but pushed the chocolate and cigarettes at him and ran blindly back to my bunk. There I pulled the blankets over my head.

The girls working in the men's camp had already heard of the night of terror. Those of my friends who had passed notes between me and my husband knew that he too had been swallowed up by those insatiable monsters, the crematorium's huge ovens, serving their bloodthirsty masters, the SS. Susan and her sister sat with me till the early hours of the morning. Nobody spoke but their nearness and comradeship was the last saving grace. It preserved my sanity.

We now had new guards in the morning but all caution went overboard. Prompted by the need to see my mother and hear her soothing voice, I did not even wait to be detailed for work but jumped straight across the fenders of the train between trucks to the basement window. My mother and many other prisoners were waiting for us and Mum threw me a loaf of white bread through the bars. We had not seen white bread since our days of freedom. But before I could speak to her, I felt a tearing pain in my left leg and turned my head to see a fierce German Shepherd with his fangs buried in my flesh. Across the fenders, a rifle barrel was staring at me. "Catch her, Ralph, catch her! Good dog, tear her up, make mince-meat of the bitch!

Good dog!" snarled the guard.

I saw my mother's white, stunned face and against the impulse to tear myself away and run from that brute of a dog, I heard Ruth's low, patient voice, "Don't ever run if an SS dog is after you. Stand still even if he has got his teeth in you and he'll let go." The voice faded away but the pain endured. However, I didn't move. The dog, as if surprised, let go of my leg and moved away from me.

The guard shouted, threatened, hit out at the dog, told it again and again to catch me; but the dog, tail between his legs, did not touch me again. The SS man pulled me roughly across the fenders, hit me over my hands with his rifle, and the beautiful white loaf dropped into a puddle of mud. He trampled it into the ground, but that was hidden from my mother by the train. That, at least, she did not see. The pain in my torn leg obscured the pain in my heart for the rest of the day. Freddy was well out of it. How long would he have suffered? A long hour perhaps, knowing he was going to die? Five minutes in the gas chambers? If anybody had given me a choice, I would have taken death and peace. Now and for many a day to come.

The day came to its logical conclusion: Report at the gate, sentence to starvation rations and hard labor for an indefinite period. Then I had to kneel on sharp stones for two solid hours, and at last, deep, exhausted sleep with legs drawn up to ease the pain of the dog bite and knees bloodied by stones.

Chapter 11

This time, hard labor consisted of digging trenches, standing up to the hips in stinking, stagnant water and hacking away rock-like soil from the embankments. The sun burned pitilessly on our bare, shaven heads; our backs creaked with the unaccustomed work. My leg was festering and suppurating where the dog had bitten me. Again I was too tired at night to eat but thirst, accumulated during the heat of the day, never left me. We were not given anything to drink from morning till night. The women around me died like flies from heat-stroke, exhaustion, fever and often because they no longer wanted to live. At first the dead were carried back to camp at night, but as their numbers grew to more than fifty percent of our daily contingent, we had to dig a mass grave at the side of the trenches and there the bodies were thrown every evening, covered with a thin layer of lime. Day in, day out, the mountain of bodies grew and with it the ghastly smell of death and decay. Still the grave was left open to receive yet more and more dead.

I lost track of time. One day followed the other in killing, back-breaking monotony. The sensation of weightlessness, detachment and unreality I had first known the day my husband and child had arrived, returned. Hunger and pain I no longer felt; only thirst plagued me beyond endurance. One day, when I thought I could stand it no longer, a group of gypsies passed our trenches. Each woman carried a bowl of water and I begged them for a drink. One of them gave me her bowl. The water looked crystal clear and I drank it to the last drop. "Do you know what you have drunk, my girl," asked one of our grinning guards. "That water comes from the swamps near the crematorium. Swamps make excellent graves. Hope you enjoyed it. Prosit."

I did not want to believe it and didn't care anyway. No water had ever tasted so good. Curiously enough, once hunger had ceased to worry me, I felt less tired and more energetic. I could sit up at night and talk to my friends; only the food they continuously tried to make me eat nauseated me. Their friendship and concern still cheered me tremendously until, one night, we sat cross- legged, ten of us, on my bunk. Ada, a fourteen-year-old Dutch girl who had joined us lately, said something quite trivial but incongruous with her age. I looked up at her and saw her eyes. It is difficult to explain what I saw. Her light brown, childish, trusting eyes had changed. There was something opaque, yet tranquil and far away in her gaze. I knew beyond any doubt that Ada was going to die. This discovery frightened me more than anything I had so far experienced and I did not want to believe what I saw. After all, she seemed strong and healthy enough sitting there, chewing away at a crust of bread. However, before the end of the week she was dead. There was no illness. She just refused her rations one night and was found in a coma next morning. She never woke up again.

One Sunday, we only worked three hours to give the guards a rest. Without thinking, I exchanged my bread ration for some green apples some prisoner had stolen somewhere. Susan chided, "Now, what did you do that for, Dannie? You need your bread. These apples will only give you a sore stomach."

"The apples are for my mother. She is in hospital with a fever and this was the only refreshing fruit I could find. She wants apples anyway," I said defensively.

"Did you get a note from her?" asked Susan, very much upset. "Why didn't you tell us? We could have visited her this morning and taken her something. She must be very ill if they sent her back from staff quarters to Birkenau. For Heaven's sake why didn't you tell us?"

"Susan, this is something you won't understand. I don't understand it myself. I didn't get a note, nor has anybody told me my mother is here. I just know it and only realized it when I bought the apples."

She only looked at me in much the same way the Blockova had done when I told her of the newly arrived transport from Berlin. Susan too seemed to be doubting my sanity but she did not want to question me further, simply took my arm in her friendly, casual way and, together, we went to the hospital barracks. We entered the isolation block and asked the first prisoner we met for my mother. We were led to a bunk near a window. There she was shivering, her face yellow and pinched, her eyes enormous and abnormally bright. Her face lit up when she saw me and she took the apples, ate one greedily and asked, "Darling, how did you know I was here? I have been lying here for the past hour thinking I'd give anything for a fresh apple and there you are, anticipating my crazy longing."

Susan pinched me and said carelessly, "Somebody from the hospital came along and told us you were here, Elizabeth. What is wrong? Anything serious?"

My mother shook her head. She had been diagnosed as having malaria. A transport of malaria patients was to be sent to a so-called research station where doctors experimented with human guinea pigs. "Don't worry," my mother said. "The SS woman in charge of this transport has given me anti-malarial tablets, and as soon as the fever is down, she is going to take me back to the staff quarters."

Already, her index card had been removed from the rest and the only reason she was here at all was that the SS doctor happened to see her when she had an attack and demanded she be sent to Birkenau. He would see her on his evening round but would not be present when the transport left in the morning and would never know she had not gone with it.

I was satisfied and knew she would be all right although Susan was still worried and doubtful when we left. My mother had noticed that I had become very thin and her last words to me were, "I'll do everything possible to get you to the staff quarters. I don't give massages and mend silk stockings for nothing. Frau Brunner, the commanding officer of all SS women in Auschwitz, has promised me she would get you over. She is a real Prussian, strict but just, and never breaks a promise. She doesn't fit into this place and treats prisoners with some consideration." My mother did not know I was condemned to hard labor and we did not enlighten her.

One evening, shortly after my mother's brief stay in Birkenau, I began feeling exceptionally light-headed and dizzy. We did not get back to camp till roll call and as usual there was no time for a wash. Afterwards it would be dark, the washrooms would be locked and again I would have to wash in a bowl of tea, the dark brew I would now much rather drink. Still, there was no shortage of tea and my friends who were not so desperately thirsty would give me plenty.

Susan and her sister, inseparable, were the first to greet me, and when I looked at the younger girl, a cry escaped me I would have given anything to choke back. In Lorna's blue, normally sparkling eyes was the same expression I had seen in Ada's not so long ago. She too was going to die. A tall, strapping fair girl now, she would be dead in a very short time. What would Susan do without her?

The girls took my arms and led me outside for the unavoidable roll call, asking me repeatedly if I could stand up and if I was feeling all right. Apparently I had turned ash grey and was shivering. They held me up throughout the parade which must have lasted much longer than usual. We were still waiting long after dark. Most of the time I drifted through clouds of blankness, until a sharp, rasping voice penetrated the vacuum. "Elimination Tests."

A gasp of terror went through our ranks and somebody's arm tightened protectively round my shoulders. "Daniella, you'll make it. Don't think at all, just jump if they tell you to. There is nothing to it. Don't collapse now, there'll be plenty of time afterwards," a voice whispered in my ears. It seemed miles away. Slowly we moved forward and, one after another, the girls in front of me took a short run, jumped, and were swallowed up in the dark, starless night.

Suddenly, I was all alone and the rasping voice said, "Next one: One, two, three, jump!" He shone a bright torch first into my eyes, then in front of me onto an open drain and a heap of sand behind it. My legs were heavy and useless and refused to move forward. I must have jumped though, for a second later I had fallen into the ditch and collapsed in utter darkness.

Torrents of icy water were splashing over me when I next opened my eyes. I was lying under a cold shower. Shivering, my teeth chattering like castanettes, I crawled slowly and painfully away out of the range of that stinging downpour. But no sooner did I feel safe when a pair of rough hands, aided by a well-aimed kick, shoved me back. Too weak to struggle or resist, I tried again and again to escape on hands and knees but to no more avail than a drowning kitten might try to get away from strong hands that held it under water, hands that know no pity or concern for another creature's suffering.

Mercifully, even tormentors grow tired of their games. Every ordeal is bound to come to an end. The first thing I knew was that I was in a single bunk-bed with white sheets and thick blankets. On a stool beside me was a small, white loaf, jam, and a mug of water. The food did not tempt me, but oh, how good it was to stretch burning, aching limbs under those clean, cool sheets.

I must have slept off and on for hours for when I woke again it was dark and the naked bulbs with their glaring light made my head hurt unbearably. Patients were called to get up and stand to attention, and from beds round about me shadowy figures struggled to stand bare-footed on the brick floor of the hospital ward.

Dr. Mengele made his round followed by a retinue of SS and prisoners in white coats. I did not even attempt to get up. My legs felt like rubber and just the effort of moving my head made me squirm and cry out with pain. A nurse pulled down my sheets and blankets and opened the coarse shirt over breast and stomach. Under half-closed lids I could see the doctor and his followers shrink back and, squinting down, I saw bright pink, round spots all over my exposed stomach.

"Typhoid," the doctor said, "immediate isolation. What crackpot put her in here?" He moved on and two prisoners, so-called assistant nurses, dragged me between them over the cold brick floor, out of the ward into another barrack which reminded me of our first night in Birkenau. With its smells, darkness and tormented screams, it only differed in that this hut had three-tiered, single wooden beds instead of bunks.

Once accustomed to the gloom, I found myself staring up to the top bed into which I was told to climb. The two nurses hoisted me up and, to my horror, I found the narrow bed already occupied. When I mentioned it to them, they said, "What do you think this is, a sanatorium? Get in." They shoved me up with a jerk that landed me right on top of the sick girl already there. She received me quite kindly and moved over but I soon found my weak apologies were not understood. The burning, dark eyes in a narrow white face belonged to a Greek, and all the girl understood was Greek. However, she motioned me to the foot of the uneven straw mattress and covered me carefully with half of her blanket. Somehow we passed the night, both of us shivering under the impact of fever.

At dawn we were wakened by wild shouts. "Get up, you filthy Bs, get up for delousing." Helping each other, we got down from our top bed and shared a bowl of cold water for a wash. Needless to say, there was no soap and no towel. While we were trying to wash our hands and faces and keep on our feet, an assistant nurse whipped down the straw mattress and blanket.

She said quite regretfully, "These have to go for fumigation and we've got no replacements. So you better get on your bunk and warm each other. Send your complaints to the management." The Greek girl did not understand a word, but prodded, she struggled back up and helped me too. We sank, arms round each other, feet intertwined, onto the bare planks, no covering except our short, rough shirts.

Nature can be kinder than humans, though. I went into a deep coma and nothing penetrated, neither the hardness of the wood nor the cold, not even the feverish struggle of the Greek girl who, another patient told me later, raved throughout the night.

I don't know how long I was unconscious but when I woke, it was with a feeling of iron bands around my shoulders and legs holding me down with a firm, cold grip. It was daylight again. I tried to move but was so weak I could barely raise my head. When I looked at the girl beside me, I screamed. Her head had fallen back, her mouth was wide open, and she stared at me with glazed, unseeing eyes. She was dead. What had felt like iron bands were her cold, stiff limbs still gripping me in her last effort

to get a little warmth. Poor child. What she must have suffered coming from her gay, sunny Greece to this prison
camp where she found only cold, calculated murder. To
her, more than to those who had been gradually prepared,
this must indeed have been hell on earth.

My screams were heard. Shuffling, indifferent
footsteps approached my bed and stopped. I called out
again and the well-fed face of a prisoner, a sick-bay atten-
dant, appeared over the side. My bed-mate's body was
soon pried loose and, with one hard pull from the atten-
dant, the corpse plunged over the side of the bed and
crashed down the three tiers onto the brick floor. The head
and two greedy hands popped up again and found
yesterday's bread ration on top of which the Greek girl had
died.

"That's always good for the black market. It will
bring at least two pieces of soap or a margarine ration.
White bread is a luxury we can't afford to throw away
with the dead. Still," said the head to me, "when you snuff
it, do me a favor and keep your bread at the foot of the bed
and don't squash it. After all, I have to carry your body out
of here. That deserves a bit of consideration, don't you
think? Meantime, you can wallow in luxury and have the
bed all to yourself. I'll try not to put anybody else in with
you." The head was in an expansive mood and talked on
and on, but in the end I heard only a far-away murmur and
must have fainted again.

Again, somebody was talking, far away. It might
have been the same voice, but no, there were two voices
and they came closer. I tried to cling to the peace of the
unconscious but something penetrated. "She is dead. No
pulse, no heartbeat. You can put number 52 in her bed.
Dump her on the floor. She won't feel anything." I saw the
Polish woman doctor, a prisoner herself, and a nurse bending over me and then moving on to the next patient. True

enough, I felt nothing until, in an aura of white light, I seemed to be looking down from a great height and saw my own body on the brick floor in the darkest corner. A huge rat was darting out from behind a corner post to settle down on my bare legs. The light vanished and all of a sudden all of me was back on the ground again. Shock and horror must have given me super- human strength. I rolled along the floor and crawled towards a bed near a window. How I got up on to the top bunk, still without straw mattress or blanket and unoccupied, I'll never know. Once that objective was achieved, I fell into a deep sleep and when I woke up, I felt well. The fever had gone and with it all the pain. Only weakness remained, but the will to survive was there again and I immediately began to scheme how to get out of the sick-bay and back to my friends. When the SS doctors visit was due, I had made up my mind.

Sick prisoners were forbidden to address the doctor unless he spoke to them first, but I was determined to appeal to him. After all, Dr. Mengele, although known as the "Angel of Death," had saved my mother in one of his rare humane moments. I could see him before he came near my bed. He glanced at his chart and asked the prisoners' senior nurse, "What have we here? I thought that bunk up there was empty." He pointed at me. "Who or what is that apparition?"

The nurse was not tall and she climbed onto a stool. "Who carried you up there?" she asked with her deep, almost masculine voice.

"I came by myself. I did not want to die in that corner."

She slapped my face hard. You are a liar. You could never get up here by yourself. You were all but dead." She slapped me again. The SS doctor stood by and watched the scene with obvious interest and amusement. This was my chance. I ignored the nurse and sat up as straight as I could. It cost me all my will power. My back muscles hardly supported me.

"Sir, there must be a mistake. I am perfectly well and have no fever. Would you please release me and let me get back to work?"

The nurse, stunned into silence for a moment, hit me so hard my nose began to bleed and would have gone on hitting me had the doctor not kicked the stool from under her feet. She rolled on the floor and, getting up slowly, brushed the dirt off her white apron. She was frightened and cowed.

Dr. Mengele came nearer my bed and shoved a thermometer into my mouth, looking at me steadily all the time. He removed the thermometer and said, "Where have I seen you before, you miserable skeleton? You have beautiful eyes . . . Wait a minute, weren't you the nurse who came with the Berlin transport in April? I thought I had sent you to Dublinka or somewhere with a malaria transport."

"No sir," I said quickly, "that was my mother. Please, will you let me get back to work?"

Again he looked at me closely. "Well, I like your courage and your eyes. Report to me when you are worth looking at again, but if you return here sick I'll kill you myself." He scribbled a note, handed it to the nurse and told her to take me to the sauna for delousing before returning me to my barrack in the labor camp. I was to have double rations and light work for two months. I was released, but the following night all remaining patients, without exception, were taken to the gas chambers. For days, the "nurses" scrubbed and cleaned the sick bay, and the fumigated mattresses and blankets were returned to the empty, silent wards.

My friends were indescribably happy to see me back. They fussed over me, offered all kind of tidbits, even shredded chicken on fried bread. The chicken, I learned later, was really frogs' legs, the only protein prisoners occasionally caught in the swamp.

Now I found out how weak I really was. The girls had to hold me up during roll calls and even the few steps from our hut to the assembly ground was too much. They carried me to and from work and during the day heaped up clothes in the barrack of the men's camp where they covered me and left me to rest, sorting my quota of clothes between them. They were very good to me.

Susan's sister was dead. She died the night before I returned from the hospital. Susan, whose courage I admired tremendously, cared for me more than anybody else. I often marvelled at her great and generous heart. She might have resented my release, physical and mental wreck that I now was in comparison with her attractive young sister. Not her. She nursed me with infinite, saint-like patience, humoring, supporting, giving hope. She re-taught me elementary knowledge forgotten during my illness. My memory failed and often I did not know who I was, where I was, and why I was there. Years of my life had vanished somewhere along the road of disease and misery. As far as she could, Susan filled in the gaps, but it wasn't until years later that my past came back to me and events gradually fell into place.

In spite of the girls' love and attention, I didn't seem to gain strength. It wasn't for lack of will power because I was as determined as ever to survive, especially in my more lucid moments. I tried hard to walk and stand on my own but my muscles simply refused to obey my will. Nor did my brain function normally. Later I was told that I had had long conversations with Lorna, Ada and other girls long since dead. Sometimes I started singing in the middle of the night, mostly cradle songs to my baby. They told me I pleaded with Freddy to take new clothes and to let me wash his old ones. I don't know how many days or weeks this continued. We had not had an elimination test for some time.

Inevitably, after a lull between transports from Germany or occupied countries, they started again, and one afternoon we were assembled and taken back to camp very early. As we approached the gate, we saw that all commandos had been recalled. We had to wait a long time to be counted and recounted before we finally reached our barrack. There, we were immediately lined up outside for a roll call. It was hot and I felt tired so I let myself drop to the ground and fall asleep. My reactions were those of a small child or a senile mind. Any urge or need had to be gratified at once and no amount of reasoning, pleading or threatening would have kept me on my feet and awake at that moment. I woke up when the Blockova kicked me and hit my face and the girls on either side pulled me up. It was too late.

The SS doctor had gone through our lines and had not missed me. Before I was fully awake, I was dragged away from my friends and joined a handful of other poor, tottering creatures. "Block 24," somebody said. A heart-rending wailing started up all around me. Within seconds we were surrounded by armed guards and their dogs but we did not move as yet. I suppose we were to wait until our numbers were complete. Again I slipped to the ground, unable to stand any longer. Nobody seemed to worry and the guards took no notice of me. Though I was weak, my brain seemed to have cleared, and once more I was able to observe with complete detachment.

One woman near me screamed abuse at a guard until she was hit over the head with a rifle and collapsed. Another fell on her knees and with outstretched hands pleaded with the guards to let her go back to the workers. She said she was too young to die and that it was all a ghastly mistake. Over and over again she repeated that she had been pretty and that she was still strong. The guards turned their back on her, nobody listened, but she went on pleading. Some prayed to a god who was deaf and blind and had forsaken them long ago. One stuffed a piece of bread into her mouth and ate it greedily as though her salvation depended on it. Mostly they cried, some quietly, others noisily with sobs that tore at their wasted bodies. There was little dignity among us and I could not bear it.

I got up and found I could stand and even straighten my back. I took the hands of two women next to me and said softly so the guards would not hear and make fun of us, "Let's make an effort and die decently. There isn't really any fun in living, is there? My husband and child were killed not so long ago and I'll be in good company. There is no future for me. How about you?"

"My parents were gassed and I don't know if my brother is still alive," said one. "My father was shot and my mother and five-year-old twin brothers were gassed," said the other. "My fiance died in Sachsenhausen. You are quite right although it seems hard. I am only nineteen." We talked for quite a while and gradually we got others to talk and it helped. Most of the women calmed down. Only the girl who was pleading with the guards was still on her knees and would not be distracted; there were two Greek girls who did not understand us, but they, fortunately, did not know where they were going and probably wouldn't know until the last minute.

We were still talking when I heard my name being called. I did not move or answer. What more could they do to me? The guards opened their ranks for Dr. Mengele and Frau Brunner, the commanding officer of the SS womens' staff quarters. They went past us, peering into each prisoner's face, arguing wildly. The doctor was shouting, "Now look here, I let the mother into the camp against all rules and regulations. I allowed the daughter out of the hospital after one of the worst cases of typhoid I have ever seen. She was a Muselman, fit for nothing but the gas chambers. In fact, she should never have been in hospital in the first place after failing elimination tests. But again I made an exception because of the mother. I promised myself and her I would see her dead if she ever came to my attention again because of ill health. Now she can't even stand through roll call any more and you come along and demand her release for your staff quarters? Have you gone off your head? Do tell me, do you intend to turn Auschwitz into a sanitarium or a holiday camp for physical and mental wrecks?"

The SS woman strode past me, turned and stopped, pointing her whip at me. "You are Elizabeth's daughter, aren't you? Same eyes, same mouth. Why don't you answer when your name and number are called?" Before I could answer, she turned to the doctor, fixing him with cold, steel-grey eyes. "I want to take this girl for the SS laundry and I want to take her now. I am not interested in any promises you gave yourself or a lousy prisoner. You know, I have full powers to demand any woman I need. The camp commandant and the labor leader have authorized me to transfer her to the staff quarters, and if you have any complaints, you'd better lodge them there."

Without taking any further notice of him, she handed a note to one of the guards, told him to get me into the sauna and out of it as quickly as possible as she was waiting to take me to Auschwitz.

The doctor turned on his heels and stormed away. My guard told me to get moving and I went under the envious, hostile and pleading eyes of those others condemned to death. What a fraud and a coward I felt and how I wished the ground would open up and swallow me. Only a few minutes ago I had asked the others to die decently and with dignity and now I was walking out on them. Once more I had cheated death at the eleventh hour. It was becoming a habit. The guard had no patience with my indecision and reluctance to move. He prodded me along at the point of his bayonet.

All the way to the sauna, on the long, painful walk to the staff quarters, and up to this day I have asked myself if I had not perhaps known I would be saved again. Could I have died decently? Should I not have insisted on going with the others to Block 24 and faced the ordeal? The knowledge of one's own selfishness and perhaps cowardice is very hard to live with.

Chapter 12

Through a haze of fatigue I saw white faces pressing against the iron bars at the bottom of a staircase. Many hands stretched out towards me and I heard my mother cry out among a babble of voices. SS Brunner strode ahead and told me to stand back. With her strong, clipped voice, void of all emotion, she ordered the prisoners to go to their dormitory immediately and stay there till she told them they could move freely again. Underneath that hard shell she had a heart, however, and she was just. She explained that disease was rampant at Birkenau, that I was probably crawling with lice, and that nobody was to come into contact with me until I had had a bath and clean clothes. She added that anybody who caught lice from me would get their marching orders back to Birkenau. She could and would not risk infection being carried to the staff quarters.

Within seconds the gate was cleared and all prisoners had vanished except the Capo of the laundry who was told to stand by with fire tongs to take my clothes and burn them immediately. This vexed me. At the transfer to the staff quarters I had been given a new dress, new, clean underwear, and stockings. How many in Birkenau would have felt the richest people on earth had they been given the chance of wearing them? Now they were going to be burnt. But I was too tired to object, and what, after all, was a set of clothes compared with the millions of human beings who had been burned in this death camp?

The long run from Birkenau had been one of those nightmares one never gets used to only, contrary to most nightmare marches from there, mine ended in what appeared to me to be heaven. All the way, the SS woman had pedalled slowly ahead on her bicycle. Like a dog, I had run and stumbled after her, always afraid that should she get out of sight, the mirage of the staff quarters and my mother would vanish again, as unattainable as survival seemed at that moment. Behind me, the guard had pushed, prodded and kicked me on. "For goodness sake, woman, can't you do better than crawl? Do you want to spend the night on the road, you miserable B? Get moving." To me it seemed I had never run so fast for so long. My sides were aching with every breath and every step, but like any other, this road too came to an end. It was a miracle I could make it at all when only a few hours ago I could not stand for any length of time.

Now I was propelled into a warm, heated shower room. I could hardly trust my eyes: I was in a small ante-room leading to the bath; both were white tile to the ceilings, the floor was tiled, there were two wooden benches on either side, clothes hooks and a mirror on the wall. The SS woman stayed outside and left the door open for the laundry Capo to take out my clothes. Etta was the sister of our Blockova in Birkenau but she was her sister's opposite. Homely, small and plump, she did not aspire to beauty. Her head was set deep between broad shoulders as though nature had forgotten to give her a neck. But how kind she was.

Her gentle voice was infinitely soothing when she asked me to undress and have a warm bath quickly so I could see my mother soon. "You know, Daniella, your mother has been a mother to all of us here but she has never been at peace. I wish you could have seen her face this morning when Frau Brunner said she was going to Birkenau to get you." With those words, Etta whisked away my clothes, careful not to touch them, SS Brunner closed the door behind her after dropping a towel and soap on one of the benches.

A person who has never been in a prison camp cannot imagine what it is like to be alone for the first time: the luxury, wonder and happiness of privacy and solitude. Nobody can appreciate what it is like to be jostled and pushed every minute of the day and night, never to have a moment of unobserved peace; to be lying like a sardine, wedged in at night, trying not to stir, trying to avoid the clammy contact of other bodies; washing and undressing in a crowd; working and standing in crowds all day long. Until this first solitary moment, I had barely been aware of my longing to be alone.

I turned on the shower and the cascade of pleasantly hot water that didn't disappear washed all exhaustion and despondency off me. The soap was real, scented toilet soap, not the evil-smelling concoction made of human fat we had on rare occasions been forced to use in Birkenau. I washed and soaked and washed again. Nobody rushed me, nobody pushed me. Eventually, Etta knocked at the door and brought in a heap of new clothes, the summer uniform of the staff quarters: a black and white, cotton dress with white collar and cuffs, a white apron and headscarf, new, clean panties and white socks. She said apologetically, "I'm afraid there is no brassiere yet. We didn't know your size but we'll fit you out in the sewing room tomorrow. The girls there will alter your dress too, if need be."

What utter bliss: a Capo who was considerate enough to knock at the door before coming in, who worried about a missing brassiere and the appearance of my dress. She left me alone again after promising to take me directly to my mother when I was ready. I turned off the tap. It seemed a lifetime since I had felt so clean and warm, but before dressing, I could not resist the temptation of the mirror. Since our deportation in April I had not had the chance to look into one.

This bathroom mirror was so high up on the wall, I

could barely see my face in it. The closely cropped, sprouting hair on my head showed a round, white spot the size of a teacup. I knew about that white hair. Susan had told me. It had turned white the night my husband and child had arrived in Birkenau. However, I was not prepared for the rest.

I climbed onto the bench and what I saw made me shudder. I had the face and body of an old woman, wrinkled, grey and sagging. I looked like Ruth, my first acquaintance in Birkenau, and so many, many others who had died or had been gassed so long ago. I resolved that my mother would never see me undressed and appreciated all the more Etta's kindness for not having remarked on my appearance. It must have shaken her, having lived so long among the healthy, well-fed, isolated prisoners of the staff quarters. I dressed quickly. Dress and apron, although a small size and too short for my height, were hanging loosely around my emaciated form. Etta pulled the apron bands tight and tied them in front to give an appearance of neatness. She then took my hand and led me to the dormitory. SS Brunner had gone, locking the entrance gate and leaving us alone.

It is impossible after so many years to describe what it was like to embrace my slight, slender mother who seemed so much bigger and stronger compared with the feather weight I was at that moment. Let it suffice to say that we talked and talked about everything and nothing. I don't think I told her how SS Brunner found me, but she must have guessed how close to death it had been. There must have been other prisoners around, but they tactfully left us alone to get over the first joy and shock of our reunion.

The dormitory was crowded with two-tier bunk beds, and how wonderful it seemed to me to have clean, white sheets and pillow cases and thick, woolen army blankets on every bed. Pipes which supplied the SS women's central heating upstairs kept it warm. But it was the cleanliness of the room that made it so striking.

My mother tried to make me lie down. Prisoners were not normally allowed to go to bed before the evening meal unless they were ill, but she was sure she could make an exception. I was too excited, however, to relax and we talked on and on until, at dusk, the front gates were unlocked and prisoners brought in loaves of bread, heaps of margarine, sausage, jam and two large containers of steaming hot tea.

Only then did the other girls turn up, clamoring to be introduced. I met them all, the women from the sewing room, the laundry, and later those who worked in offices. The latter were extremely lovely girls, chosen I think for their beauty rather than their knowledge of office routine. There were one or two, in fact, who were semi-illiterate. Curiously enough, they were the ones who looked down on washing and sewing women and kept very much aloof. On the whole, the prisoners of the SS staff quarters were a confined, artificial community, a caricature of a purely feminine society with all its snobbery and prejudices. The "upper class" was represented by the office staff, the "lower class," with all their ready kindness, willingness to help and their enjoyment of gossip, by the sewing room and laundry women.

All this I learned gradually, but one thing was obvious from the start: the prisoners here were civilized human beings. Probably due to their softer living conditions, they could afford to respect each other's privacy and individuality. There was no fighting or pushing for food. Everybody waited patiently in line until their turn came. The Capos did not take the best part of the others' rations. There were no arguments over beds, blankets and the rotation for baths. Everything was arranged justly and without friction and one never awoke to find a bread ration or other treasure stolen.

It was strictly forbidden here—as it had been in Birkenau—for prisoners to own any personal property but it was amazing how much was collected just the same. Every girl owned a small bag made from remnants in the sewing room which contained everything from a little, cracked mirror and broken combs to last year's diary and stubs of pencils found in the SS women's wastepaper baskets. Prisoners who worked as chars upstairs brought them down. Every girl owned at least one handkerchief and a table napkin. During the day, such treasures were hidden in the straw mattresses and at regular intervals were found during the meticulous searches by the SS women on duty. Yet within a few days everybody had managed to replace their lost possessions.

How delighted I was to find a bag of red and white gingham on the bed allotted to me next to my mother's. It contained a small mirror, a comb with only one tooth missing, a handkerchief and a toothbrush. I had no hair to comb yet and did not want to look into a mirror ever again, but the very knowledge of owning such treasures made me feel rich.

My mother made me some dainty tidbits from our evening rations. Laid out on a napkin, white and clean as fresh snow, were paper-thin slices of bread with finely cut pieces of sausage and small triangles with jam. The tea was hot and sweet. Safe and contented, I felt hungry for the first time in weeks and wolfed down my delicious supper. There was plenty of everything left and I asked for more but my mother knew only too well the danger of overeating after a long period of starvation.

For the first time in her life she refused me food although it was there. I behaved like a spoiled child, pleading and begging for more and refusing to take no for an answer. Fortunately, the whistle for roll call interrupted her agony and my further disgrace.

What a different affair the roll call was here compared with Birkenau. All we had to do was to line up in the warm passage outside the dormitory. We were quickly counted by the SS woman on duty and told to go to bed. The whole affair lasted barely three minutes.

My mother tucked me up in bed as though I were a small child again. My stomach was still rumbling but I was so warm, clean and comfortably drowsy, I no longer minded the hunger pangs and fell asleep within seconds. In the morning I awoke refreshed. Fresh air and sunshine entered through the open windows, only iron bars casting shadows on the floor. Birds were singing in the trees outside. It was the sweetest music on earth. Although we were confined to the basement and never got out for exercise, I was perfectly content for the moment just to be there. Compared with Birkenau, this was peaceful and luxurious living.

Breakfast had been prepared for me and my mother had not only managed to toast the bread somewhere before I woke up, but also to produce a cup of real, hot, sweet cocoa like a magician whisks a rabbit out of a hat.

After breakfast we were counted again. The office staff had already left but we did not have far to go. Just along the passage was the sewing room which contained a few long tables, wooden chairs and some old, decrepit sewing machines. In spite of the open windows, it smelled dusty and it was rather dark. My mother and the others turned in and I just had time to see a heap of silk stockings in front of my mother as she sat down, her dark head barely showing over the top.

The laundry was a long room further on. There were three large boilers and three long, wooden troughs with washboards. There was also a small tub where the best of the laundresses washed the SS women's daintier clothes separately. Etta detailed me to one of the long troughs and to a washboard somewhere in the centre on the far side, my back to the window.

"That's the best place for you meantime," she said. "You can sit on a stool till you get stronger and get up if an SS comes in without being noticed. If you can't cope with your allotted washing, pass it on to your neighbors. They'll do it for you." She must have noticed me wince for she added kindly, "No need to feel ashamed, Daniella. We were all weak when we first came from Birkenau. If we had not been helped to start with, we wouldn't be here now. Just take it easy and you'll be surprised how quickly you'll pick up." She went off to stoke the fires under the boilers and distribute the day's quota of work.

Etta was one of those rare Capos, non-existent in Birkenau, who worked as hard as any of her girls and didn't mind helping out at the washtubs if we did not manage to complete the ordered quota. We had to do the washing of all SS officers and guards from Birkenau and Auschwitz. The SS women's washing was only an infinitesimal part of our duties. The male guards' shirts and underwear were so dirty you would never have guessed they had once been white. Etta grabbed them with the fire tongs, as careful not to touch them as she had been with my clothes yesterday. After mixing lots of soap powders in the boilers, she dumped everything in, closed the lids, wrinkled up her nose in disgust and said, "Well, that's that. Filthy swine, this master race." She then distributed the men's long underwear, pants, vests, shirts, grey tunics and socks as well. Although these had been boiled the previous day, they were still unbelievably dirty. With soap and scrubbing brushes, all severely rationed out, we were to get them clean and spotlessly white again.

Every night our finished washing was inspected and if

there was the slightest dirt mark still visible, they were thrown back at us with threats varying from withdrawal of rations to transfer to Birkenau. The girls told me nobody had so far been sent back except for serious infection. Whenever a transfer was ordered because of complaints on the work, SS Brunner always overruled the orders since she had the last word. However, you could never trust any SS woman, and one day she too might be in a bad mood and let us down. The threat and fear of Birkenau hung forever over our heads.

The whole of that first day, I don't think I managed to clean even three shirts. Towards early afternoon, after a good lunch of stew and potatoes, the other girls had reduced their heaps of washing to almost nothing and mine was still as big as ever. Yet, my back and arms ached unbearably, and in the end tears started rolling down my face and I just couldn't stop crying. My neighbors at the trough grabbed the rest of my washing quickly and divided it up and down the line. In no time at all it had vanished.

The Dutch SS woman, who had been in the men's camp with us in Birkenau, did the evening inspection. She hardly looked at our efforts and said to Etta, "Everything finished, Capo? Have you done my blouse and undies today?" Etta lifted a bundle of pressed, neatly folded clothes off a stool behind the boilers and handed it to her. The SS woman gave us a bright smile. "Thank you girls, have a good night." Before she left, she came over to the trough, gave me a curious, compassionate look and asked, "Are you Elizabeth's daughter? How do you get on with the washing? You don't look strong enough."

My neighbor on the right poked her elbow in my ribs and answered quickly on my behalf, "She is doing fine, Aufseherin (Overseer), she finished her whole quota. She is much stronger than she appears to be." The SS woman shrugged her shoulders, grinned doubtfully and disappeared.

The day's washing was collected, hung up in the drying room, and we returned to the dormitory, supper, roll
call and bed. My mother told me later that the Dutch SS
woman was the best of the lot. Mum had massaged her
once for a stiff neck and mended her stockings and ever
since hardly a day passed that she didn't come down to
bring my mother something to eat. Today she had left a bar
of chocolate and three cigarettes. My mother didn't smoke
so I shared them among the few girls who did. We had half
a cigarette after supper, enough to make me lightheaded
and dizzy again.

The Dutch woman's story was the old one of a beautiful girl from a poor home who fell in love with a good-
looking SS officer in Holland after the German invasion.
Her father kicked her out when he learned of the affair and
so she had followed her lover to finally end up in
Auschwitz. Unlike others, she never got used to cruelty
nor did she herself take to the perversions usual amongst
the SS. Naturally, she did not like what she saw in Birkenau, but she was a superficial, fun-loving creature, popular with men for her good looks and gaiety. She was
always given the best and healthiest commandos of
women prisoners and on the whole managed successfully
to close her eyes to the horrors around her. Very occasionally she had black moments of despair. When she did, she
sent for my mother under the pretext of needing a massage
for a sprained ankle or knots in her shoulder muscles, and
then she almost cried her heart out.

Unlike us, who were afraid of the present, she was
afraid of the future. She was intelligent enough to see the
way the tide of war was turning. "Elizabeth, what am I
going to do after the war? I can never go back to Holland.
Where else could I live? Would anybody anywhere ever
believe me that I did not kill or torture prisoners?

Elizabeth, you are a nurse and know about drugs. Tell me the best way to kill myself. Shall I do it now or when the war ends?" In that vein she talked on and on. It was a monologue and did not really require an answer. My mother felt sure the young butterfly would not kill herself and did not take her very seriously. Contemptible though she might have been, she was one of the very few, if not the only one, of our guards who was kind to us and treated us as individuals. I had done her an injustice in Birkenau when I had thought she was keeping her mouth shut about our meeting men because she was well paid. She accepted presents as a tribute or flattery, but was perfectly capable of deep affection for a prisoner like my mother who had nothing material to give.

Chapter 13

The office staff returned for their evening meal and brought back with them the latest gossip from the outside world and from the other prison camps their offices administered. "The war is nearly finished," they said. How often we heard and how often were still to hear this prophecy. Here, in the staff quarters, we could afford to be a little more patient. The prisoners in Birkenau could not. There, the daily ration of hope, dealt out by a few courageous men who tried to keep up morale with facts or fiction, had ceased to mean anything to desperate people. Nobody knew whether they would live a few more months or merely hours.

However, in the winter, when the tide in Russia really turned, we were jubilant. Big or small, every event brought to us from the outside world was magnified. Sitting on our beds at night, we debated every development. We arranged the affairs of the world for the next century to come. There was no doubt in our minds that the few who would survive the terror of this decade could convince any government on the globe of its past and future mistakes and so prevent their repetition in the lifetime of our children. In our analysis of the news, we broke through the restrictions of imprisonment, and the barrier of years and confinement was, temporarily, less irksome.

Preoccupied though we were with the future, our first aim was to get as many prisoners as possible transferred from Birkenau to the staff headquarters. With the "shoe commando," passing prisoners, and the office staff came many desperate messages pleading for help. Our chance came eventually, but first these comrades of ours had to face yet another winter under inhuman conditions—a winter in Birkenau that demanded a heavy toll of lives.

As the German offensive in Russia came to a standstill and then turned into a fast retreat, there were more and more reprisals on the helpless, suffering inmates of the concentration camps. Many new transports arrived, mainly from Hungary, escorted and handed over to the SS by their own Hungarian militia and police. Theresienstadt, the camp in Czechoslovakia where distinguished families from Germany had been sent because of their past services to Germany and had lived under bearable conditions, was dissolved and the inhabitants evacuated to the gas chambers of Auschwitz. So ended the lives of our most famous contemporary scientists, doctors, musicians, university professors and other distinguished men and women who had been too loyal, too old, or like my father, simply incapable of believing the Germans would condone mass murder.

This journey in cattle trucks from Czechoslovakia to Poland was Germany's return for a lifetime of faithful service. After they were all gassed, they still brought a last, involuntary service to their beloved fatherland: their gold teeth, rings and medals, even their hair were removed from their bodies and sent back home.

Every setback in Russia and North Africa was marked by mass eliminations and the gas chambers again worked day and night. There was a rumor, later confirmed, that gas and room for this planned genocide were in short supply and people were burned unconscious but still alive. By order of our camp commandant, gas was no longer wasted on babies and young children. They were thrown alive into the ovens of crematoria and open bonfires.

I recovered quickly. In a very short time I filled out

and grew strong again under my mother's loving care and supervision, helped by ample food. Soon I not only managed my daily quota of washing but could help others as my neighbors had helped me. The day came when I risked another look in the mirror and found that I looked young and pretty again. My hair had grown nearly two inches and was standing up like the prickles of a hedgehog, but with patient combing and brushing it settled down silky and boyish.

Early in winter, a rumor that we were soon to be moved to a new camp at Auschwitz was confirmed by SS Brunner. She said it was a very nice building and a great improvement for us. However, proposed changes in a concentration camp were always dreaded. So many promises and false hopes had been dangled in front of prisoners' eyes and had ended in misery and death. A deep depression settled down on us, and as the days shortened and the sun no longer penetrated into our basement abode, we appreciated more and more how snug and warm and comparatively safe we had been here. The Dutch SS woman cried when she learned of the impending move and that did not help to reassure us. As it turned out though, she cried because she had come to rely on our company in her darker moments of fear and on the comfort of having her clothes cleaned, mended and looked after without having to exert herself.

The day before my birthday, on December 27th, our dormitory was again searched and raided and all our little possessions disappeared from under the mattresses. We had just been given half of a Red Cross parcel each for the first time. So far, everything sent for prisoners by the International Red Cross had gone to the SS. My share had contained, among a few other things, a can of sardines and some chocolate biscuits. I had kept them unopened with the intention of giving a birthday party on the 28th. They had vanished with my other treasures. So I sat on my bed and cried. The girls laughed at me. They had been there long enough to know they would soon replace their losses, but I was still new and the things taken were my first possessions since my arrest. What hurt me the most was that I was now unable to do something nice for my comrades who had been so good to me. Nobody else had had sardines in their parcels and everybody's eyes had popped out of their heads when we unpacked them. Gone!

My mother was called upstairs again after roll call to massage the Dutch SS girl. Some of my friends said, "Don't go, Elizabeth. Punish her and say you are not feeling well or something. She only wants to cry on your shoulder. Rub it in that they have taken all we had, even Daniella's Red Cross parcel." But my mother went upstairs just the same. I was asleep when she returned.

She woke me with a kiss and said, "It's your birthday, my darling. You know, all the things I wish for you but, more than anything else, freedom and happiness." Before I was completely awake, I was hugged and kissed by everybody. I rubbed my eyes. On a stool at the side of my bed was a tray with twenty-one burning candle ends and, laid out on my mother's already neatly made bed, were presents: a new bag embroidered with my name, a comb, a hardly used toothbrush, a handkerchief and a napkin with my initials, a bar of chocolate, ten cigarettes and a can of sardines.

The girls stood back to watch my reaction. I could not help it; I broke down and wept. No presents in the past or in the future have ever touched me the way this unexpected surprise did. During the night, after I was asleep, the girls had sat down to sew and embroider the bag, handkerchief and napkin after raiding the sewing room for material. The comb and toothbrush came from a girl whose bed in a corner had been overlooked in yesterday's raid. She would now do without till she found new ones. The candle ends were stolen from the SS women's Christmas tree by prisoners who had cleaned upstairs, and the chocolate, cigarettes and sardines were a contribution from the Dutch SS woman after my mother had told her of my distress.

"A twenty-first birthday is a very special one," somebody said. "You have now reached the age of discretion and can use your inherited fortune as you please without asking your mother's special permission. You are free to do with your life whatever you want. Use your freedom wisely. Bless you."

We all burst into helpless laughter and the day was the best I spent in a concentration camp. Working hours passed quickly and in the evening we all sat cross-legged on the beds and celebrated. The candle stumps were lit again and we each had a square of white bread with a sardine, a piece of chocolate and half a cigarette. Chocolate and cigarettes had been augmented by the office staff who had "organized" some during the day. Never had a can of sardines stretched so far and given so much pleasure. About thirty of us were sharing my bounty. I was rich.

Sometime in January, SS Brunner took the Capos of the sewing room and laundry to look over the new camp and work rooms in order that they could assess the number of prisoners to be asked for from Birkenau and what additional equipment was needed. Both Etta and the other Capo had recently managed to get their sisters transferred to us and the two sisters took over for the day they were to be away on their inspection tour.

Our ex-Blockova couldn't curb her deep, commanding voice and hearing her shout all day brought back unpleasant memories. It also made me realize what a fine person Etta was. However, the sister's bark was worse than her bite. On the whole, she had changed for the better.

She soon learned that she no longer held power over life and death and that she had to behave herself if she did not want to be ostracized. Her sister had a calming effect on her too, but she still never learned to share equally in our working life; she gloried in her position as second-in-command and was never popular. If Etta was ashamed of her, she only showed it by working harder and helping us more and hid her distress even when she was nagged by her prettier, younger sister. Our ex-Blockova was by no means the worst, but to a certain extent the SS had achieved their objective in making her a tool, an almost incorrigible camp product.

The two Capos returned radiant and full of good news. Sitting in our usual position, cross-legged on our beds in the evening, we listened unbelievingly to their reports. They had decided on the way that Magda, the sewing-room, elder Capo, would tell us first about the living quarters and Etta would then take up the story and tell us about the new place of work and her proposed requirements.

Magda's smiling, dancing eyes were infectious. "Listen girls," she said, "try to imagine a newly built, two-storey house with lots and lots of large windows, no iron bars, and a staircase in the centre. Downstairs, a large common and dining room on one side, tiled showers and toilets on the other. Upstairs, two big dormitories on either side of the stairs, each containing well-spaced-out, double-tiered beds, tables and chairs. Believe it or not, there are woven mats on the floor around the tables and each bed has sheets, pillow cases, blankets and an eiderdown quilt."

Here she was interrupted. "Stop kidding, Magda. We'd swallow the story about the beds and tables, but when it comes to floor mats and quilts, we draw the line. Come on, be fair." But she insisted there really were eiderdowns on each bed. We let it pass and presumed fresh air and unaccustomed walking had gone to her head. She was a quiet, not easily excitable Hungarian in her thirties.

She went on raving about this new building of ours, one of four identical ones, surrounded by similar houses which were, at the moment, vacant. Later, they were to house passing army troops on their way to the Russian front. There was no electric fence and no watchtowers round the new camp, only a single, ordinary, wire enclosure. My ears pricked up.

The four houses reserved for prisoners were going to be shared out as follows: House No. 1 for prostitutes to keep SS, army, and privileged German prisoners amused, and No. 2 for office staff working in the so-called "political department" and camp administration. No. 3 was intended for laundry and sewing room personnel. "No. 4 is a mystery," Magda frowned. "It is a house just like the other three but completely surrounded by barbed wire, a camp within the camp." SS Brunner had said we were not permitted to go near the barbed wire of No. 4 and anybody caught speaking to the inmates there would be sent back to Birkenau immediately. We were allowed to visit prisoners of Houses 1 and 2 although No. 1, she hoped, would not be frequented.

We debated for a while who the prisoners in No. 4 would be, but as nobody had any likely solution, Etta took over from Magda to give us an idea of our future working conditions. The laundry and sewing quarters were about a mile from camp but it was a pleasant mile through fields and tree-shaded avenues. Etta wasn't quite sure but she thought it was outside or just at the perimeter of the watchtowers, very near the town of Auschwitz. The buildings must once have been a small factory. They were built around a cobblestone yard and there were stables and administrative blocks on one side. The laundry was huge and would easily employ fifty to sixty girls. There was a drying room, large enough to warrant at least two or three permanent attendants. The place where clothes were pressed and mangled would require another twenty workers and the sewing room about thirty. At the moment, the laundry and sewing room together employed only about twenty-five prisoners and that meant we could safely ask for the transfer of eighty to one hundred girls from Birkenau. "Write out a list, girls, of any friends you still have there and I'll present it to SS Brunner tomorrow." We cheered with joy.

"There is one more thing that might interest you. There are men from Auschwitz, mainly trusted old prisoners working in the stables and administrative buildings of the factory. They drive horses and carts into the town with only one guard and trade for food for the SS kitchens. We didn't get a chance to speak to any of them today. You know SS Brunner and what a stickler she is for proprieties and ladies' decorum." Etta grinned. "No doubt we'll get the chance to make our neighbors' acquaintance. Now get on with your lists of likely transfers."

I waited until everybody dispersed. There were things you didn't discuss in the presence of office staff employed in the "political department." Two of them we suspected of being planted spies for the SS. That was never proved beyond doubt, but one of them had been at one time the most notorious Capo in Birkenau. She was killed at the end of the war by a few survivors she had maltreated there. While she lived with us in the staff quarters, she was always trying to be friendly, too friendly, and nobody trusted her or spoke to her more than was absolutely essential. The other was her right hand—to her, subservient, to the rest of us, arrogant. We feared and disliked these two.

As soon as they were out of sight and hearing, I went after Etta and asked her what had been uppermost on my mind. "Etta, what are the chances of escape from the factory?" Maybe she wasn't the right person to approach on this subject. She was rather more timid than the rest of the Slovaks. The laundry was now her life and I often suspected that, in her zeal to do well, she forgot who she was working for. Escape had certainly never crossed her mind. Nevertheless, her answer to my question was sensible, much as I disliked hearing it.

"If we were in Czechoslovakia or even Germany, Daniella, I'd say go ahead and try if you can bear the thought of reprisal and torture on the wretches you left behind. However, as long as you are in Poland, you haven't a chance in hell. You know what happened to nearly all the Jews who escaped through the sewers of Warsaw? The Poles will hand you over to the SS without batting an eyelid. You haven't money or jewels to try and bribe them, although they'd probably take that and still return you. Only if you want to commit the most horrible and painful kind of suicide imaginable should you try to escape from Auschwitz." She put her hand on my arm. "Have a little more patience. The war is bound to end soon and, judging by the standards of our new camp, you have every chance to survive."

A week or so later we moved, once again losing most of our collected treasures. We were not allowed to take anything from the staff quarters save the clothes we had on. Most of us concealed combs and toothbrushes in our bras, risking the possibility of being stripped. We were not and this time got away with it.

It was a beautiful morning when we marched out of the staff quarters for the first and last time. Just the same, hearts were heavy, for this building had been shelter for a long time and the future was frightening. Even prisoners are creatures of habit and we were frankly afraid of any change.

Chapter 14

We arrived at our new quarters and a united shout of joy soared into the still, blue sky. Lined up in front of the house were our friends from Birkenau. Etta had given SS Brunner our list and since then we had heard no more about it, but here they were, Susan and many others. They were ghastly thin, pale and shivering in spite of the sun. Many faces were missing, but those that were there were so happy to be away from Birkenau at last that I felt bitterly ashamed for our reluctance to leave the staff quarters. We were immediately allowed into the building and nobody very much regretted the departure of the office staff into the adjoining house.

Inside, it was just as Magda had described it, bright and airy, with mats on the floor and eiderdowns covered with satin in matching colors on each bed. Unbelievable luxury. For the girls from Birkenau who had, all this time, slept on bare wooden or brick shelves, it was an even greater change and surprise. Many of them wept with joy. The excited chatter stopped and for a while there was utter and complete silence when everybody thought of our many friends who had not survived the last bitter winter in Birkenau and the forsaken thousands who still existed, doomed and without hope, in the death camp. Nobody had said "three minutes' silence." We were so adjusted to our common fate and tuned in to each other's thoughts that it was seldom necessary to make an announcement.

About lunchtime, the prostitutes moved into house No. 1. They were a lot of beautiful young women in gay, colorful coats, a noisy, chattering crowd. Few wore make-up and, had we not known who they were, they could easily have been mistaken for students and factory girls which, of course, many of them had been in their former life.

Later in the afternoon, the last house behind barbed wire was occupied. We walked around it, curious to find out something about these confined neighbors, but SS guards drove us indoors. We did see, however, that they were all young, Jewish women whose hair was neither cut nor shaved and that one of them had a little boy of perhaps four years of age with her. He was the first young child I had seen since I entered Birkenau.

Just before roll call, one of our girls got a chance to speak to them. They were the human guinea pigs we had heard about, women who were subjected to the most cruel experiments since the Middle Ages. Some were sterilized, others had animal sperm implanted, many were operated on without anesthetic or pain killer of any kind. German "doctors" performed bone and skin grafts on them and transfusion of incompatible blood groups. Some were submerged in freezing water and given large amounts of salt water to drink while the "medical team" watched to find out how long it took them to die. The resulting knowledge was intended to aid naval rescue. The woman and her child, Peter, had come with a fairly recent transport from Berlin. Because of her beauty, she had been given the option to volunteer as a guinea pig and so save her child. She had not hesitated, although she was probably the only one who knew what she was letting herself in for.

Most of the occupants of this "research laboratory" were newcomers whose trials and tortures had only just started or were about to begin. Those of their group who had already been experimented on and who were of no further interest to the SS doctors had been taken to the gas chambers of Auschwitz.

Susan and a few others sat on my and my mother's beds that evening. They were not in as bad a state as I had been. To the last they had been fortunate enough to work in the storehouses of the men's camp, but even there food had become scarce during the winter and they now greedily ate the sandwiches we made for them.

The news they brought from Birkenau was terrible. Since the first rumors of Allied victories in Russia and North Africa, the SS had doubled and tripled their extermination program. Again, the gas chambers were working around the clock while transport after transport was fed into their gaping doors. Any time there was a short pause between arrivals, Birkenau had to provide the numbers to keep them going, and elimination tests had become increasingly more frequent. The SS made no secret of their intention to exterminate every single prisoner should Allied victories continue.

Meantime, we learned that our new camp had been erected as a showpiece to the world. Its gates were to be thrown open to the Red Cross for inspection. Hence the eiderdowns, the mats on the floors and the luxurious, tiled shower room.

At 9 p.m. the lights went out, and soon the dormitories were quiet except for the regular breathing of the sleeping inhabitants. I lay awake thinking over the reports from Birkenau and marvelling at some of the girls who had joined us today. I had seen them praying before going to sleep. How could they still pray after all they had just seen? I envied them their steadfast faith and trust in some divine justice.

Eventually I too felt drowsy and was just dropping off to sleep when I felt a small hand glide under my blankets and rest on my breast. A voice whispered, "Daniella, darling, you are beautiful, beautiful." I got hold of the hand and, careful not to waken my mother and my neighbors, climbed out of bed and dragged the hand and its owner to the window. In the faint light of the moon, I recognized a fourteen-year-old girl who had been in our transport from Berlin. Frozen to the ground, she looked up at me terrified.

"Don't hurt me, please don't. I can't help loving you. I was so longing to touch you." I took the little thing by the scruff of her neck and shook her, but soon under her lack of resistance my first unintentional fury spent itself and I let her go.

"Don't ever do that again, you silly thing. Learn to control yourself and don't corrupt others." I steered her back to her bed, tucked her in and went back to my own, shaking with repulsion, but I sooned learned that some of my best friends had become lesbians in Birkenau. Their attachment and love affairs with other girls were their only escape from reality and the terrible strain of existence in the death camp.

The little girl who had come to me had been seduced by older women before she had had a chance to know a normal life and real love. Once I realized this, I tried to talk to her and help her sort out her mixed-up feelings and desires, but I don't think it did any good. My initial disgust and brutal reaction had frightened her so much that I could not penetrate her defensive attitude.

Prisoners, men, were walking in and out of the new laundry. Nobody stopped them, nobody questioned their business. The guards and their dogs who had escorted us to the "factory" had departed and the Dutch SS woman sat with a book in a warm corner of the sewing room. The men brought us some of their washing wrapped around packets of margarine, salami sausages, sugar, or pieces of cheese. They seemed to have plenty of time for they talked to us for as long as an hour. Soon, friendships developed between them and the girls and the same men always brought their washing to the same women. Of course, there weren't enough men there to supply all the girls with washing and I was glad nobody had singled me out yet.

I felt shy all of a sudden and had forgotten how to talk to a man. At least I thought I had, until one day a man arrived at my trough and spoke to me. He was a gorgeous creature, tall and good looking, witty, friendly and polite. He talked to me for a long time and only then asked if I would do his washing for him.

"You are a great lady; I hate to ask you for this service, Daniella," he said with old-fashioned and, under the circumstances, ridiculous courtesy, "but you know how hopeless and helpless we men are. Anyway, if you would do this for me now, I promise you will never do a washing again in your life once the war is over. You'll have servants and all the luxuries you were surely accustomed to before the war." He was a fast worker and I had a proposal of marriage before the day was done.

The sad truth was, however, that this charming man sometimes thought that he was Siegfried the dragon-killer, sometimes King Louis XIV and sometimes Napoleon. On days he was Louis, his personality was the most delightful and intriguing. I always looked forward to his French days. He spoke the language fluently and pretended he didn't understand German. It helped to brush up my French and was great fun. The peculiar thing was that he never appeared ridiculous, and in whatever role he happened to live he was a gentleman. All the girls adored him and nobody made fun of him. He must have been about twenty-eight or thirty years old and had been in various concentration camps for more than ten years. His way of escape was enviable and his personality so commanding that not even the SS molested or ridiculed him.

We had far more work than we ever had in the staff

quarters even though there were now so many more girls. Now that we had more personnel, more space, and more equipment, the SS piled it on. Previously, we had washed for officers, SS women, and a few privileged guards; now we got the washing of all guards stationed in Auschwitz, Birkenau and round about—truck loads full of the filthiest clothes imaginable. Our food got worse. In the staff quarters we had received leftovers from the SS; here it came from the camp kitchen of Auschwitz and was often as bad as it had been in Birkenau. Again, rations were kept back by the Blockova, a German political prisoner, and her house service staff. By the time they reached us, they were reduced to the most minute portions. The long, brisk march to and from the "factory" and hard work made us terribly hungry. Therefore the food wrapped in the men's washing was more than welcome even though it meant scrubbing all day long without a break, even through lunch hour. It was hard living, but in comparison with Birkenau it was still heavenly.

Not all girls from our commandos were fortunate enough to get the washing of prisoners and I know many were so hungry they sold their bodies to the men for a piece of bread. There was plenty of opportunity for them to slip out into the stables whenever the Dutch SS woman was with us and that was most of the time. Thus most men had two girlfriends: one who washed for them, another as an outlet for their desires. They were going to marry both after the war. Among the girls there was jealousy and pathetic fights over their lovers. The men, of course, told each one what she wanted to hear. To the one washing his clothes he would say, "Because I love and respect you too much, I could not bear to touch you until we are married, but you must understand the needs of a man. You are too innocent, darling. As long as some women can be bought, that innocence will be protected from our baser desires."

To the other: "I love you more than anything in the world, but a man has to get his washing done, don't you see?" These affairs were parodies of the eternal triangle behind barbed wire. I don't know whether my Louis XIV did the same, but then I did not imagine myself to be in love with him and was quite disinterested in his amours.

During the day, I hardly saw my mother, but at night we shared what rations I had managed to earn with the extra washing. Women in the sewing room did not see much of the men and had less opportunity to work for them. Once their clothes were torn, privileged German prisoners got new ones and did not bother to have them mended. So I was very surprised when my mother brought back a whole liver sausage one night and I teased her unmercifully. When she did get a word in edgeways, my surprise was even greater.

This welcome contribution to our scant rations had come from Otto, the men's Capo. We all knew him by sight, but he was the only prisoner who never entered the laundry or spoke to any of us, although he always gave us a friendly wave when we arrived at work in the morning or late at night.

Now he had unprecedentedly strolled into the sewing room and sat down on the table in front of my mother, swinging his long legs. He had asked her where she came from and complimented her on her youthful appearance. He told her he had been in concentration camps since 1933 for his part in a street brawl with Nazi troopers before Hitler came to power. The murder of two SA men could not be pinned on him but, as he was a communist, he was arrested as soon as Hitler was prime minister. Somehow, somewhere during those years, the reason for his original arrest was forgotten. When prisoners were classified into political and criminal groups, he preferred to wear the green triangle of the criminal on his sleeve. He thought his chance of survival in that category was greater.

He never spoke of his past, only the future, and in the beginning I could not understand why he had singled us out from all the others. It was soon obvious that he loved me deeply and revered my mother. He was wise to the dangers and pitfalls of concentration camp life and knew instinctively which guards and SS women could be bribed to turn a blind eye. When he looked aloof and turned his back on us when we arrived at the factory, we knew, that a dangerous guard was on duty and that it would be a day we could not talk to each other. How I missed his considerate, loving kindness on these days. Yet, I never imagined myself to be in love with him and in any case knew too much about the dangers and heartbreaks of love in a concentration camp to easily permit myself the luxury of feelings.

One day he showed me a pouch. It had been concealed between the false bottoms of his desk drawers. It was brim full with uncut diamonds. "These will buy our freedom soon, little Daniella." However, his plans to escape did not materialize. He contemplated many different ideas, but in the end was always defeated by Polish hostility towards Jews. Escape from the factory would have been easy enough. All we would have to do was to hide until the workers had left at night and then walk out as soon as it got dark.

Occupied now with their own fears and problems, many guards had become careless and often we were not even counted before returning to camp. At roll call somebody could have answered for us when numbers were called and it might have been possible to deceive the SS until the more thorough counting in the morning. Otto could easily have escaped on his own. He was a German but spoke Polish fluently and was, unmistakably, not a Jew. However my mother and I would have had little chance to get even as far as the German border. We would have had to travel by day as well as by night; for by morning our escape would have been discovered, and unless we had moved a considerable distance, dogs would track us down with the ready co-operation of the Poles. We pleaded with Otto to take his chance and go alone, but he would not be persuaded and was determined to see us through.

Chapter 15

Winter turned into spring and spring into summer. The fields we passed on our way to work displayed their poisonous green. Even the trees had none of the tender colors of spring you see anywhere else in Europe. What was there about Auschwitz that turned even nature into something ugly and deadly?

Time passed quickly enough. We were working harder and harder. I was now posted to the drying room where it was hot and comfortable, but as it had no windows I worked in artificial light all day and hardly ever saw the sun. I could not work for my favorite prisoner any more either. Otto kept us well supplied with food, but I missed the delightful conversations with "King Louis XIV."

Through Otto we heard of political developments, but we could not really rejoice as every Allied victory cost thousands of lives in Birkenau. The nearer Germany moved towards ultimate defeat, the greater the lust for mass murder.

The barracks surrounding our buildings were now fully occupied by soldiers passing through to the Russian front. On their return they rested there for a week or more. There were wounded; we got their washing too, and often the water in our troughs turned red from the blood caked on their uniforms. We now worked day and night shifts. More women were transferred to us from Birkenau. All ex-staff quarters prisoners worked night shift and slept in the daytime.

In the summer of 1944, we saw Russian bombers passing over Auschwitz for the first time and then heard the rumble and explosions of bombs dropping on the nearby town. We learned from Otto that the underground workers of the resistance had passed on detailed maps of the layout of concentration camps in the area to the Russians. They had a secret transmitter operating somewhere in the men's camp. Otto now stayed behind in the evenings and talked to us for a while every night. I don't know how he wangled this extra time at the factory, but I suppose diamonds were sufficient persuasion if paid in the right quarters.

One lovely summer day, I could not sleep and sat on a window sill sun-bathing. At the window in the barracks opposite were a few soldiers. One was playing an accordion and the others sang, mostly wistful tunes of home. I closed my eyes to listen and basked in the warm sun. From time to time the soldiers stopped singing to shout to me something like,"Hello, beautiful, this is a request program. Any songs you would like to hear?" I ignored them and did not answer. So they just continued with their music.

A sweet, sentimental song was interrupted suddenly by a mighty roar in the sky and, looking up, I saw it was black with low-flying bombers. It was like a bad dream when their flaps opened to emit small, oblong, black shapes. A carpet of bombs fell towards me.

It can only have been seconds between the time I saw them and the blast. One minute I was sitting on the window sill in the sun, the next I was flung against a bed post; everything was black with clouds of dust and breathing was almost impossible.

When the dust settled, I glanced out the windows. The sky was clear and blue again and there was not a single airplane to be seen. But the soldiers' music had stopped. Where their barrack had been there was a deep, gaping hole and a heap of rubble. With all these bombs, only the one building had been destroyed, but in the fields and yard around it there were innumerable craters.

My mother and most of the other girls had been sound asleep when the force of the explosion threw them out of bed. They got up, rubbed their eyes and shook the dust off their clothes. They looked as though they had been dipped in flour. Somewhat late, the air-raid alarms went off and everybody ran down to the cellar for shelter; that is, everybody except my mother and I.

A few minutes later we heard the planes roaring overhead again. This time I did not wait to see their flaps open but dived into my bed, pulling the blankets over my head. Muffled, through my covers, I heard my mother pleading with me to come down to the cellar. "You go down if you feel safer, Mum. I prefer my bed. We can only die once, and I'd much rather stay where I am."

She left me and walked towards the staircase when an explosion rocked the building. A tremendous weight settled on my chest and I choked, but a few minutes later I risked pulling down my blankets. There was a deadly silence and the sun hit my eyes at an unusual angle. As soon as I got accustomed to the bright light, I saw why.

My bed, which had been near the centre of our dormitory, was now the last in a row. The outside wall of our house had collapsed down and inwards, and I was lying on overhanging floor planks, open to sun and wind. The top bunk of my bed had partly broken down on top of me, but otherwise I was all right. As I carefully crept out from under the debris, I saw my mother limping towards me. The blast had thrown her down the stairs but she got away with bruises and a slight shock. When she saw me alive, color returned to her chalk-white face and she smiled with relief.

Only then did we hear screams from the cellar and raced downstairs. We had to break in the jammed door. It was a sorry sight that met us. Just a few of our girls were standing near the inner door. Bloodstained and shocked, they scratched away at the rubble of bricks and beams that had fallen on the rest. With our bare hands, we worked and dug and carried away the debris to uncover a few more of our comrades who were badly hurt but still breathing. Two hours later we had finished. We found ten dead and many of the others so badly injured they had little chance to survive. There were many more with broken bones.

Those of us who were not hurt worked on and on, and with superhuman effort carried the injured out into the fresh air and as far away from the building as we could. The dead we left behind. When the next wave of bombers approached, we broke through the single strands of wire fencing and ran into the open field, panic stricken and without thought of consequences.

Not a single guard or SS man was anywhere in sight. Squadron after squadron of Russian bombers passed over, dropped their loads and disappeared again. By the time they had finished, there was not a single SS or army building left. They were razed to the ground, but, except for the one stray bomb that had hit the wall of our house, the prisoners' houses were untouched. The Resistance workers' plans of the prison camps and the SS barracks had been accurate.

During the lull in the attack, we carried our wounded into the field and there we sat or paced about unmolested for at least an hour after the last raid was over. Then, slowly and cautiously, SS guards appeared at the skyline of the field. From behind trees and bushes these heroes approached, their guns pointed at us. From a safe distance they shouted at us to line up and raise our hands above our heads. We did, except for the wounded who could not get up or lift their arms. From an easy shooting range, the SS fired at our injured and we ran back through the fence to our damaged building, dragging with us those unable to walk and not yet dead. From then on we were locked in the terrifying cellars during air raids, but since all SS targets in our immediate neighborhood were already destroyed, we were never under direct attack again.

Exhausted after this eventful, sleepless day, our decimated commando was marched out to work at night, and when we arrived at the "factory," Otto was waiting on the steps of his office, his face white and strained. The news of our dead and wounded had already spread to the men.

He did not even wait until the SS woman had vanished to her place in the sewing room, but raced through the laundry into the drying room. Without bothering to shut the door, he gripped my shoulders so hard I thought he was going to crush my bones. For once this cool fearless man lost all control and cried like a tormented child. "If anything had happened to you and your mother, I would have killed myself." It was the nearest he ever came to actually saying that he loved me. Unlike the other men who tried to tie girls down, he never asked for promises or emotions, although he was ready to risk his life for me.

By early October 1944, there was no longer any doubt about the final outcome of the war. Through Otto we got all the information received by the Resistance on the movements of the Allies. It was now just a matter of time until the Allies would meet on German soil. But if outsiders thought Germany would realize its defeat and capitulate, we knew better. After eleven years of Nazi terror and nearly five years of war, not even the enemies of the Nazis realized they were dealing with unpredictable madmen. We, their victims, knew only too well.

The wildest rumors circulated among us: the whole of Birkenau was going to be liquidated; the last transports were arriving and after the prisoners were gassed, all traces of the death camp, the grave of millions of Jews,

Russians, Poles, Czechs, Hungarians, Greeks, French, Dutch, Gypsies, and Germans, was to be obliterated.

Otto gravely confirmed these rumors, but he was convinced that, this time, the SS would not succeed in carrying out their plans. The Resistance, now very strong in most camps, would save the prisoners of Birkenau. So we were not surprised when the word passed that prisoners of the "Sonderkommando" (special commando forced to gas, cremate and bury the victims) had revolted at last and blown up the gas chambers with bombs smuggled in by partisans. Before they exploded, rumor said, the prisoners threw into the vaults as many SS guards and dogs as they could get hold of. We all had come too far to think of possible reprisals. Without reservation, we rejoiced in the knowledge that the tortured prisoners of Birkenau were at last free of these monstrous, smoking death chambers and that the men had, at last, fought back and refused to kill their own people.

Two days later Otto brought the terrifying news that something had gone wrong and only one of the gas chambers had actually been destroyed. The SS had sent reinforcements as soon as the explosion was heard, and all existing Sonder-commandos had been gassed. The revolt had failed. The murder continued on a larger scale than ever before.

Smaller revolts continued for a while. The bloody, scorched and bullet-holed uniforms of SS guards sent to us for washing bore witness to the courage of desperate prisoners. But those fighters were doomed from the start. Contrary to regular German army units, the SS could still draw on almost unlimited reserves. Reinforcements flooded into Auschwitz to carry out reprisals and put down any spark of resistance. Even our guards were increased and became watchful and vicious once more. We were counted and recounted innumerable times every day. The men could no longer stroll into the laundry and bring us their washing, and even Otto rarely managed to talk to us.

At the end of November he appeared in the drying room. His face was drawn and tired. He had bribed one guard and made the other so drunk with illicit alcohol that he would be unconscious for the rest of the day. Nevertheless, his voice held tremendous urgency.

"Daniella, this is the last time I can talk to you. All German prisoners are going to be transferred back to Germany tomorrow. We have the option of volunteering for SS or the army. The latter means the Russian front. All my men have volunteered, but I prefer to stick it out to the bitter end as a prisoner and will probably be sent to Dachau. All that, however, is beside the point—just for your information. I want you to listen very carefully to what I have to say. Your life and your mother's may depend on your memory. All healthy prisoners, men and women, will soon be evacuated. You will most likely be sent to Belsen. I shall try to tell you what is probably going to happen.

"You will get five minutes to assemble and, surrounded by guards and dogs, you will be marched out of camp. Soon, on the main road past Auschwitz, you will be joined by endless columns of prisoners from Birkenau and other surrounding camps and more and more SS. The march will be very fast because the Russians will be close at your heels. It is winter and it will be bitterly cold. Now I am coming to the points you must remember if you don't want to die within sight of freedom and victory. Don't let your mother get out of your sight, no matter how hard the pressure from behind. Keep to the centre of the column, no matter how fast you are made to walk. Never get to the front or sides. When prisoners get tired and slow down, the guards will shoot and club to death anybody within their reach in the front and flanks.

"You must promise me to stay somewhere in the centre, will you? No matter how tired you are, don't fall behind. Push on and grit your teeth.

"If the pattern of previous transports I have been in is followed, the women will have a cart in the rear to carry those unable to walk. Don't feel tempted to get on it and don't let your mother get on even if you have to carry her. Those on the cart will be killed somewhere along the road.

"I don't know how long you will have to walk. It might be only hours; it might be days; it might be weeks. Remember what you have been through already and don't give up so near the end. No matter how weary you are, Daniella, go on."

I stood mute as he took my face tenderly between his hands. "Daniella, I have never asked you for any promise. I have never asked you to love and to marry me. I'll see about that when I find you free after the war, but now I am asking you to live. Will you promise me? If I never saw you again in my life, I could not bear the thought of a world in which you and your mother did no longer exist. Promise me, Daniella, promise, please."

"I will live," I promised.

"All right, pet, let's presume you saw a chance to escape the first night. Don't try it on Polish soil. You know what happened to others who tried it, and don't feel tempted to make your way to the Russians either even though the front may be very near. My sympathy has been and always will be with the Russian struggle for survival, but the Russian fighting forces are a rough and mixed crowd, brutalized to a point where rape and murder are everyday events. You don't speak Russian and couldn't even explain where you came from, should they wait for an explanation from a beautiful young girl, which is unlikely.

"Curb your impatience until you get well into

Germany. Then make a break at your first opportunity. The chance will come your way, and when it does, don't hesitate. Believe me, I have thought about the wisdom of giving you this advice through many a sleepless night. I know it is dangerous, but Belsen is worse. You may survive even that notorious camp, but your mother would not. If she got as far as Belsen, she would look so old and frail from the hardships of the journey, she would be sorted out and killed on arrival. She would not be allowed even to enter.

"Can you remember all I have told you so far? It is vital." He repeated it all and asked me to tell my mother everything except the necessity of our escape. He thought that would worry her and frighten her so much it might sap her strength before we even started.

"Keep that extra burden and responsibility to yourself and take the initiative when the time comes without unnecessary explanations. Your mother will follow you wherever you go.

"As soon as I have gone tomorrow, you must go to my office. I have arranged with the Dutch SS woman that you are to collect some papers from my desk. Under a loose floorboard behind the door, you will find a pair of fur-lined shoes for your mother and skiing boots for yourself. You will need them. Wear them from now on so that they are well worn and comfortable when you are evacuated. There is also a pair of long, warm trousers there. Take SS sweaters, warm underwear and another pair of slacks from the drying room within the next two weeks and wear them under your striped prison garb. See you get a complete and very warm outfit for yourself and your mother because you will have to take off the striped uniform.

"Your mother told me once you have friends and money in Berlin. Get there as quickly as you can and always keep close to the crowds of German refugees who are bound to be on the road fleeing from the Russians. Don't stay in Berlin either. There will be a lot of bombing and fighting before the final crash. Make your way to the West and wait for the Americans and British. They won't be long.

"This advice is all I can do to help you. I could give you some diamonds, if you want them, but I would advise against your taking them. You and your mother are so damned honest, any ape could read in your faces that you carried something valuable. Also, you have neither the experience nor the mentality to bribe the right people at the right time. You would be far better to join the stream of refugees, destitute as most of them will be. Look after your mother, you sweetest girl in the world." He turned and almost ran out of the drying room and laundry. I did not see him again as a prisoner. The following day the "factory" was deserted. All German male prisoners had been evacuated. Their transport had left Auschwitz by train early in the morning.

It was lonely after he had gone, so terribly lonely. And I was again terrified of the future and my responsibility. Only then did I realize how much I had come to depend on and lean on Otto. He was wise and kind, at least twenty years older than I, and for the second time in my life I felt I had lost a father and the first security and protection I had known in years of struggle and misery.

There were other changes too. The German Blockova had been evacuated and replaced by a prostitute. Food got scarcer and no extra rations came our way. The Dutch SS woman who had been so kind to us left with a transport for Germany and we had a succession of cruel, sadistic women. SS Brunner still protected us and took an interest in our welfare from a distance so guards were forbidden to beat us, yet we got kicked and slapped in the face for crimes as insignificant as an unwashed SS handkerchief.

On return from work, we were locked up in camp and could no longer walk around the yard or talk to girls from the other buildings. All that was bearable. We knew it would only be a matter of time until something happened. We waited.

Many of the girls hoped the Russians would liberate us overnight, before we could be evacuated. I did not. I was afraid of the Russians and even more afraid of being killed by the SS before we fell into the hands of their enemies. And, curiously enough, in spite of all that had happened to us, I was homesick for Berlin as I had never been before.

Years ago, when the Gestapo had finished with me, I had fervently hoped I would never see that accursed city again. Now I was breaking my heart with longing to get home. I never mentioned it to my friends for they were all Zionists. For them, Palestine was home. I wanted to share their enthusiasm for I knew full well that I could never live in Germany again, and I was afraid that for the rest of my life I would be a stranger wherever I went. I hated everything German but loved the soil and the beauty of the country with all my heart.

Only days after Otto left, I stole a pair of navy blue, woolen slacks and a brown pullover from the line in the drying room, put them under my striped uniform and rolled up the trouser legs. I looked and felt somewhat bulky. For days I was frightened, waiting for enquiries, but the clothes were never missed. Emboldened by my success, I stole more every day. Once I took a blouse belonging to an SS woman still on duty, but when she came looking for it, I quickly returned it the next day and said it had been overlooked. I got my face slapped for that but it was worth it.

Gradually I acquired civilian clothes not only for my

mother and myself, but for all my trusted friends. I could not get shoes for them but at least they would all be warm and have a chance to escape in civilian clothes when the time of transfer came.

Chapter 16

January 1945: we woke up to the steady whining of shells and the crackling of machine gun fire not far away. It was very exciting. Never did we dress so quickly and carefully. Both my mother and I put on two sets of woolen underwear, blouses and sweaters, two pairs of stockings and woolen socks. Fortunately, Otto's boots were large enough to be still comfortable.

It was bitterly cold, snow had fallen inches thick through the night and as we lined up in the yard for the usual roll call our breath froze and tiny icicles formed on our noses. A large number of SS guards carrying full marching kit and armed to their teeth turned up with the dogs and we knew before we were told that the time for the dreaded exodus had come.

The SS women did not take time to count us, and as Otto had predicted, the first group of one hundred prisoners marched out of the camp within five minutes. We were assembled in lines of four and told to wait. We waited and waited. One of the SS women used this time to search the prisoners in front. With fear and shock, I saw her tear off clothes we had so carefully collected, and the heap grew of pullovers, slacks and warm underwear she took off the shivering girls. The SS woman hurled insults as well as her whip at the unfortunate prisoners in the front who stood all but naked, defenseless under her assault.

She had almost reached us in the centre of the column when a messenger arrived with a note. She nodded and said to the messenger, "All right, thank you." Then she turned to us, lifted her whip and broke it into small pieces, grinding the remnants into the snow with the heel of her

boots. Putting her arms round the shoulders of two prisoners nearest to her, she addressed us.

"Girls, I just got a message. We are too late to be evacuated. The Russians are very close and we are more or
less surrounded. We are now all in the same boat and have
to make the best of it. I was forced into the SS and did not
want to come to Auschwitz. When the Russians arrive, I
want you to confirm that I have never been cruel to you
and have only done my duty.

"You will do that, won't you, my dear girls? Oh dear,
what am I thinking of, leaving you out in the cold so long,
you poor things. Quickly, get back into the house and
warm yourselves. Put extra coal on the fire. We might as
well wait in comfort."

As we filed in, she went on talking to us individually,
pleading with us to help her. In return she would demand
food, clothes and money for us from the Russians. I saw
with glee that the heap of warm clothes she had taken off
the prisoners had vanished and all were dressed as before.
We pressed round the stoves and nobody listened to the
continuous whining of the SS woman deploring her fate.

Half an hour later though, a second messenger turned
up with another note. Unbelieving, we saw that wretch
take up the handle of a broom to hit out at the girls near
her. "Downstairs, you pigs. Line up in marching order and
be quick about it. I'll show you what's what, you filthy Bs.
We are going back to Germany."

To escape the swinging broom handle, everybody
rushed downstairs and out of the building, but before I
could take my mother's hand, the beastly woman lifted her
booted foot and kicked her so hard in the back my mother
rolled down the stairs head first. Rushing after her to help
her up, I swore to myself I would kill that SS woman with
my own hands if I were ever free.

This time it took only seconds to line up and we were

.t of the gate and on the road before we fully realized what was happening. My mother was not hurt by her fall and that was a blessing for it wasn't a march, it was a run. In our warm clothes we soon felt too hot and were sorely tempted to take some off. For half an hour the guards whipped us on. Then we came to a short halt on the main road to Auschwitz where long columns of prisoners were plodding along, blocking the road. We by-passed them across a field. Already many of the prisoners were faltering and falling behind, and some of their dead were lining the road. The living were hit, kicked and pushed by their guards and some stretched out their hands to us, begging for bread. But we had not been given any rations this morning either and couldn't help.

Soon we left them far behind. We had the advantage of being a smaller group and physically fit. After another half hour or so, we passed a deep ditch and a gasp of horror went up from the girls on our right flank. My mother and I were in the centre of the column and did not see anything, but those who did recognized some of the first hundred prisoners who had left our camp earlier this morning among the dead bodies filling the ditch. They were mainly from the house behind barbed wire, the guinea pigs.

When the message had reached them that Auschwitz could not be evacuated, their guards had lined them up along the road, shot everyone and fled.

Was that the end we were coming to? On and on we marched; we left the sound of front-line fire far behind until it diminished to a distant, low rumble. Gradually our pace slowed down and the first moans were heard. Some girls had sore feet, others were getting hungry. At least we did not suffer from thirst. There was plenty of snow. All day we marched without break or rest until it got dark. Then the guards herded us into a deserted barn. They were too frightened of partisans, said to be hiding in the forests, to drive us on in the dark.

The barn was full of straw and comparatively warm. Exhausted, we sank down against the stacked bales. So far, our group had no losses but many had feet that were so swollen their shoes and boots would not come off. Somebody asked me if we should try to escape in the night. There was a small trap door at the side of a bale of hay where we might be able to squeeze through. Remembering Otto's advice, I refused to consider it, but two Polish girls got away while we were asleep. As we were no longer being counted, the guards did not notice their absence.

At dawn we were again driven out. If anything, it was even colder than yesterday. None of us had any food. We stuffed our mouths full of snow; snow was our breakfast, our lunch and our supper. That day we had our first casualties. Some girls had not been able to get their shoes on again in the morning. Their feet were swollen beyond recognition. They wrapped rags round their feet, but this was no protection against the deep snow and icy roads. Soon their feet were bleeding and they fell behind.

The road led through deep forests and the SS were hysterical with fear of partisans. Every time a twig snapped or a load of snow tumbled off the tall pine trees, they let off wild shots and started shooting into our ranks to speed up this nightmare march. In front, at the flanks, and in the rear, prisoners slumped down, shot in the back. Closing the ranks, others stumbled over their bodies.

Again we were on the road all day, and when it got dark we were driven into an open field, fenced in by barbed wire. There was no house, no barn anywhere in sight. My mother told everybody to keep on their feet and walk around, but mostly the girls took no heed. They were too tired to care. My mother went from one to another trying to rouse them, but in the end she gave up and concentrated on me, for I too had reached that state of exhaustion when I dropped off to sleep against my will.

The snow was soft and inviting and I curled up in it. The next moment my mother gave me a stinging slap in the face and brought me back to my feet and to my senses. I, who had promised Otto to look after my mother, was ready to give up, and my mother, with super-human strength and energy, kept me awake. Throughout that endless night she told me stories, rubbed my hands, slapped my face and back and made me run up and down the length of the field. Only a few of our closest friends stayed awake with us. When at last a pale, wintry sun rose behind the forests, those who had gone to sleep in the snow were dead. Hundreds of prisoners from Birkenau had marched throughout the night and caught up with us that morning to swell our ranks, but from our camp only a few survived.

Once more we walked all day. Many a time I would have fallen behind or dropped down had my mother not pulled me forward, her small hand round my wrist like an iron band. Hungry and tired, we stumbled over our own feet, fell in snow drifts, and went on without conscious thought. My mother's unbreakable will and wiry strength kept me and a handful of friends alive.

Finally, on the evening of the third day, we reached a railway siding and were loaded into open coal wagons, a hundred women to each truck. There was no room to stretch or even sit down. Two guards and their dogs occupied more than a third of the truck. We crouched close against each other as best we could, and with rumbling stomachs and frozen limbs, watched our two guards settle down under thick blankets and warm furs.

Each SS man took a long drink of brandy from his flask and ate chunks of bread and corned beef. Under our hungry eyes they stuffed themselves and then threw bread and meat they did not want over the side. The train moved slowly, stopped again and then chugged along steadily until, perhaps an hour later, at the German frontier, the guards' identities were checked and they received new rations of bread, sausages and alcohol. Some prisoners begged for a drink or a piece of bread, but the border guards ignored their pleas. The guards emptied their bottles in one short session and rolled under their blankets, covering their dogs as well.

Crouching there, I fell into brief spells of fitful sleep. Every few minutes somebody tried to extricate an arm or leg from the general entanglement. It was agony, but after a few hours, moving my aching legs, I woke my mother. It was almost pitch dark except for a faint glow from the snow on either side of the rails. My mother tried to move and everybody else woke up. Some cried with pain, cold and hunger; others cursed and fought desperately for a little bit of room. The guards snored noisily under their blankets and the dogs did not stir. Slowly the train rumbled through snow-covered land.

"We must be very near Kattowitz," my mother whispered. "I know every inch of this country, I was born near here. Little did I think I would ever travel through it under these circumstances. I'd give anything to be free and see my parents' house once more. Do you remember our garden, Daniella? You played hide and seek behind the hedges when you were a little girl."

"Why not, Mum?" I whispered back. "We'll get off the train here and visit your old home."

"Don't joke, darling." The guards did not stir. They were dead drunk and sound asleep. I got hold of Susan's hand and squeezed it. "Sue, my mother and I are getting out of here. Come with us." I whispered to some other friends, "We are going to my mother's home. Will you come?"

Tears were streaming down my mother's face. "Don't take any notice of her. She has gone out of her mind, my poor child."

Somebody cried out in despair and agony, "Stop pushing, I can't stand it any longer." I clouted her lightly over the head and said, "Will you be quiet, you goat. Don't you understand, I am going to make room for you now."

Susan was the only one who understood I was in dead earnest. She pushed and rammed herself to the side of the truck, pulled me after her, and I in turn pulled my mother over the crouching bodies. "Climb on my back, Dannie," Susan breathed quietly. "Climb out first and I'll help your mother once you are out. I won't come, but thanks for the invitation. You are better off on your own. There is no safety in numbers. Good luck."

I climbed on her back, swung myself over the side and jumped off the slow-moving train, landing softly in a snow drift. I waited, immobile. Almost immediately my mother followed, but she was stiff and above the noise of the train I could hear her feet clanging against the metal siding. If the dogs started barking, the game would be up.

The loud beating of my heart drowned out all other noise for a moment. In the milky glow of the snow in a foggy dawn, I saw my mother jump. She fell and rolled down a gently sloping embankment a little distance away. I ran to her, got hold of her hand and we raced over a short expanse of snowy field into thick, dark forest. We ran and stumbled through thicket and undergrowth. We fell into holes and scratched our faces on low branches and went on running till we both dropped down in a hollow.

From the direction of the train came weird noises. The engine whistled and puffed to a halt. Brakes screeched, dogs barked, SS guards cursed and shouted. We could hear it all echoing through the silent wood. I closed my eyes wearily. They were after us. There was no point in running any further. If the dogs were loose, they'd catch up with us. Our only chance was to sit quietly and motionless and hope they would not pick up our scent. The shouting grew louder, prisoners screamed and shot after shot was fired. I was paralysed with fear. Suddenly all was silent again; a complete and utter silence. The engine of the train snorted and puffed and soon the wheels rattled noisily on, westward into Germany.

We did not move until the last, distant rumble was swallowed up in the early morning mist. Then we jumped up, fell into each other's arms, laughing and crying at the same time. We were free, free, free. There and then we tore off the striped prisoners' uniforms, buried them under two or three feet of snow, and walked away in civilian clothes through the calm, glistening winter wood. Our hearts were so full, we did not speak, just plodded on, the pale, rising sun on our backs.

"Wait till we get to the next village, Daniella. I'll be able to tell you then where we are exactly and which way to go."

"Do you really want to go to your old home, Mother?" I asked. "People might recognize you. If you could bear to bypass it, we could get back to Berlin sooner. I think we should go there as quickly as possible." She agreed and admitted it was just a dream and she did not really want to see her house again. Her parents were dead and it was just as well to forget the past.

Out of the forest, we came into a small Silesian village. We were afraid to enter in case we were questioned, but after nearly four days without a bite to eat, we could not afford to walk past. For a long time we looked at the snow-covered thatched roof of the nearest farm. All the houses seemed dead. Not a wisp of smoke came from any of their chimneys, no dogs barked, there was not a soul to be seen anywhere. As we cautiously approached the farm, we heard cows mooing and rattling in the byre, but it was not the gentle sound of happy, contented animals. The noise they made was savage, full of fear and agony. I opened the gate and went in. There were only three cows and we could see at a glance they had not been milked for at least a day. Their udders were swollen to the bursting point. We found a dirty bucket and I went into their stable and milked them unskillfully but effectively. The cows seemed to appreciate my efforts. They stood quietly and nuzzled my hand in a friendly way when I had finished. We drank some of the fresh, warm milk and then went into the house.

Nobody answered our knocking. The farmhouse was deserted, but on the table in the kitchen we found bread and butter, cheese and jam, and dirty dishes. The owners appeared to have left in a hurry. We sat down and helped ourselves to some food, made a few sandwiches, and wrapped them in a newspaper that was lying around, its headlines still promising final victory.

We opened the gate of the cow shed and untied the animals in the hope they would find relief if they were free to roam. The whole village was the same: cows chained and unmilked, houses deserted, untidy and uncared for. We came to a small railway station. It was locked but a notice in the entrance proclaimed, "All train services for civilians to Berlin and West Germany will cease to function as from 2 p.m. this afternoon, the 25th of January, 1945."

We had lost track of time, but eventually we worked out that the 25th was yesterday. We had escaped on January 26th, 1945. Seven years before, on the same day, my father had died. It seemed a lifetime ago. My mother thought of it at the same time for she went on looking at the notice in that railway station and said quietly, "If I had known seven years ago all that would happen to us, I would not have grieved so much. He could never have survived Birkenau-Auschwitz. He had a wonderful escape too."

Chapter 17

The silence in the deserted village was shattered by distant explosions and even while we were listening, the noise of shell fire and cannons came closer. We had escaped from the SS, death marches and concentration camps for the time being, but we were only at the very start of a long road to freedom. We had many, many weary miles to go yet. We plodded on, following signs to the west, through vast forests, deserted villages, and frozen fields, with the low rumbling of the Russian front in our rear.

Toward late afternoon we saw the first signs of life and soon we caught up with long treks of refugees. Cart after cart blocked the road. A few were pulled by tired horses but most were pushed by men and women. The carts were loaded high with furniture and household goods, and on top of these perched small children and very old people who could not walk. These people were too preoccupied with their own plight to ask us questions, and I spoke to some of them to find out where they were going and what they thought their future was going to be.

The general feeling was that of despair, disillusionment and fear. They knew, at last, the war was lost and they had lived too close to the Polish border to have much hope of returning to their homes and farms. A few had relations in the west, but the majority was bound for Berlin where they had been told they would find shelter and soup kitchens.

It was not necessary to ask them what they thought of their "Thousand Year Reich" now. These arrogant Germans had come a long way indeed.

Unhampered by luggage, we left the trekking families behind, and at nightfall reached a large village where people were pushing toward the station. We were told there were still trains running from here and soon we joined an orderly line outside rows of ticket counters. Repeatedly the crowds were addressed and reassured through loudspeakers, "Keep calm, keep order, don't panic. Everybody will be evacuated."

Closer and closer we moved to the ticket office and it occurred to me that we had no money for the fare when a woman in front of us cried, "I have no money. I don't know where my husband got to. I lost him in the crowd but he said he'd meet me in Berlin should we get separated. I forgot to ask him for money and papers. What am I to do?" She was quite hysterical until a stationmaster put his hand on her shoulder and told her to stop worrying.

"There are hundreds like you without money and documents, old girl. We'll see you get the train all right. If you don't find your husband before then you will be given money and accommodation on arrival in Berlin. The trip is on the house. Don't you think we have deserved a little joy ride?" he said flippantly.

We finally arrived at the counter. I dabbed my eyes and cried too. "Mother and I have lost our money. I don't know where my father got to. Can you help us?"

"Sure girlie, don't you fret. Here is your ticket. See you get something to eat before you get on the train. You look hungry. It might take a day or two before you get to Berlin, conditions being what they are."

We moved on to the platform and another lineup. Grey-clad women ladled thick, steaming potato soup into big mugs. We drank our soup greedily. It seemed ages since we had anything hot and it was years since we had eaten anything so good and rich.

The train we were to board had just steamed into the

station and was almost empty. We sat down on adjoining seats. Gradually the compartment filled up, small children were lifted into the luggage racks and people sat on the floor and on suitcases all along the corridors. Doors slammed and the train moved out. My mother, I knew, was thinking as I was of the thousands of starved, frozen prisoners from Birkenau and Auschwitz travelling through the cold, dark night in open trucks, towards yet another concentration camp that few of them would survive. There was no pity left in my heart for these dispossessed members of the master race now travelling with us on this comparatively comfortable train. My eyes closed. With the rhythmic singing of the wheels, "Going home, going home, free, free free; going home, going home . . . ," I fell asleep, my arm around my mother's narrow shoulders.

It was broad daylight when I finally woke up. We were travelling through flat country. We fought our way to a washroom. Water was scarce, but there was enough for a drink and to wipe our hands and faces.

"Should we be asked our names and where we came from," my mother whispered behind the locked washroom door, "say the name is "Doverg" and we came from Kattowitz. There are lots of Dovergs there. It's a very common name in Silesia. We'll stick to our Christian names and our own birthdays so we won't have too much to remember. Should we be asked what Kattowitz was like before we escaped from the Russians, let me do the talking because.I know the town well and heard a bit of what was bombed there last night from some refugees."

We returned to our compartment to share the sandwiches we had taken from the farmhouse yesterday, but the packet, wrapped in newspaper, had vanished from the seat. Somebody had stolen them and there was no point in asking the refugees. Whoever had taken them would have eaten them by now. We were hungry, but life in

Birkenau and Auschwitz had gradually conditioned us to take losses in our stride.

The train was desperately slow. It stopped every few miles for no apparent reason. Often we seemed to go back the way we had come, and many a time we had to be shunted back and forward onto a different line to avoid craters blasted into the railroad during recent bombing. Late at night, the train pulled into Berlin. I strained my eyes for familiar landmarks of the city that I thought was like none other in the whole world. But it was under complete blackout and I saw nothing.

The station from which we finally disembarked could have been any station. In gloomy semi-darkness we could see just the bare skeleton of what were once walls of glass.

Again, crowds of refugees were channelled quickly and efficiently into orderly lines and again we were met by grey-clad women handing out mugs of hot soup. The soup eaten, we moved on to another woman who wore a big swastika badge and was asking the people ahead of us for their identity cards. My heart was in my throat, but I heard a number of them say they had lost or left behind their documents in the rush to get away.

Our turn came, we told the same story, the woman nodded and filled in temporary cards for us: "Elizabeth Doverg, born January 1st, 1902, refugee from Kattowitz" and "Daniella Doverg, born December 28th, 1922, refugee from Kattowitz."

"Have you any money?" she asked in a monotonous, disinterested voice. We said we hadn't and she gave us twenty marks and told us to report to the nearest labor exchange the following day where we would get more until employment could be found for us. "There is plenty of work clearing rubble," she confided, before passing us on to a housing officer.

"Have you anywhere you could stay in or near

Berlin?" was the next routine question.

"Yes, we have relations who are expecting us," I lied.

"Thank God for that," sighed the woman. "You are lucky. Most of these people will have to sleep in bunkers and air-raid shelters. Do you know how to get to your relatives?"

"Yes, thank you." We were dismissed. Outside the station were a few battered, old taxi cabs, all driven by women. We tried three, but were refused when we admitted we could not pay with food. Many refugees had brought something edible from their farms. "Well, if you can't give me butter or meat—even bread would do, or flour—you'd better walk. Money is no good to us these days." In the end we found one driver who asked how much money we had. "Twenty marks? It will cost you all of that. Twenty marks don't even buy half a pound of butter now."

We agreed to give her all we had and she drove us to the district where Margaret lived. We stopped and got out a good mile from her house to make sure we were not being trailed.

It must have been in the early hours of the morning when we rang the bell on Margaret's door. "Who is there?" she asked cautiously through the keyhole.

"Open up, Margaret, please, Elizabeth and Daniella here." The door flew open and closed behind us. Margaret, in an old-fashioned flannelette nightgown, danced round us like a buzz saw. She asked no questions. In no time at all she had set the table and was feeding us royally. She gave us the first cup of real hot coffee we had tasted in years. While we ate and drank, she made up two beds with our own sheets and eiderdowns she had kept for us, warmed with hot water bottles.

"Get to bed, children, you look like you need your sleep. Your story will keep till the morning and we'll discuss your future then. Have a good rest first. Oh God, I didn't think I'd ever see you two again." She laughed and cried, but all the time she was busy making us comfortable. She tucked us in like children and, with exhaustion and the comfort of a warm bed, I slept at once.

In the morning I heard whispers. "Elizabeth, where is our baby and what has happened to Freddy?"

"Dead. Don't mention them when Daniella wakes up. She has suffered enough, poor child." But I was awake and tears started running down my face. I buried my head in the soft pillow, trying to sleep again and pretend everything had been a bad dream. It was no use. I had to get used to the facts and face the future, no matter how bleak and empty it appeared.

My mother had saved my life over and over again. I owed it to her not to break down now. I waited till Margaret had regained her composure. She had genuinely loved my child and had risked her life trying to save her. It was not her fault her plans had failed. I pretended to wake up and Margaret ran a bath for me. After I had wallowed in it for half an hour she called me for breakfast. In spite of shortages, she had everything—fresh coffee, eggs, sausages, bread and butter, marmalade and jam.

Nothing had changed in her house. Our carpets on the floor and all the furniture I had given her before my attempted escape were just as I had seen them two and a half years ago. It was good to be in a real home again, but I realized that we could not stay here. I had left all my personal clothes with Margaret too, but she had sent them to East Prussia to save them from the bombing. The Russians would probably find all my lovely dresses, coats and shoes. Still, we had lost so much, what did it matter?

Margaret suggested we call in a very good and trusted friend of hers before we discuss our next move. That friend had lots of relatives in the West and might be able to help. I longed to see our old home, and leaving my mother to tell Margaret something of our experiences, I went out for a walk.

The house of my husband's parents was only a few blocks away but, although I had found Margaret's home in the dark the night before, I did not recognize a single street.

I walked in the direction of my own home, which had been taken from us in 1939. Black ruins and heaps of rubble blocking road after road were all that was left of a once-prosperous area. Taking many a wrong turn and climbing over mountains of stones, I eventually found it. The walk, which before the war would have taken no more than fifteen minutes, took me nearly two hours.

I don't know what I had expected to find, but when I faced my home, reduced to a hill of bricks and boulders, two of the hall's marble columns still sticking out of the rubble, I cried. I was crying not for the house, but for what it represented to me—my lost childhood, the ruins of my past. It made me realize how truly homeless and rootless I now was.

My school opposite the park still stood undamaged. It looked grey and tired. Against my will, my feet carried me over to its ancient portals, and as I gazed up at it, the school bell sounded as it had rung for me so many times only a few years ago. Children came running out and skipped down the granite stairs. I could not help staring at them. With an aching heart, I wished the clock could be turned back and I could be one of them again: innocent, free of the dreadful knowledge of death and destruction, free of the memory of their fathers' guilt and crimes.

One of the senior girls stopped and asked me if I was waiting for someone or if I had lost my way. I shook my head and said, truthfully enough, "I was just looking at your school. I knew a child who had been very happy here once."

The girl gazed at me uncomprehendingly. "How could she have been happy in this ghastly, antiquated dump? I wish a bomb would drop on it. The people are fighting for their destiny and still we have to go to school."

I did not wait for more slogans from this teenager. I made my way back to Margaret's. There were few people on the roads, and those I met were all women, drab and tired, scuttling like grey mice through the ruins.

My mother was frantic with worry when I got back. I had been away so long and I had to promise not to go out again on my own. Charlotte, Margaret's friend, was already there. A slender, attractive woman, about thirty years of age, she wept bitterly when Margaret told her briefly of all that had happened to us.

"Oh Germany, Germany," she cried in genuine despair, "we have deserved everything and more that is coming to us." However, as soon as she got over the first shock of Margaret's revelations, she got down to discussing with us our immediate future.

"You have to get out of Berlin as soon as possible," she said. "There are so few houses left standing, you might be discovered in the routine searches for accommodation. Also, the bombing goes on and on. If these madmen continue much longer, we will be living under siege. No, you two have suffered enough. Get out while you can. Now, let me think for a moment."

Charlotte stared out of the window for a while and nobody spoke. "I have got it," she said at last. "I am going to send you to my cousin Mahlmann in Mecklenburg. She is the stupidest female you have ever met and a great Nazi to boot, but if I give you a letter and tell her to take you in, she will. I'll say that you, Elizabeth, are my best friend and that I used to spend many happy holidays with you in your grand home in Kattowitz. I'll tell her she owes you all the hospitality she is capable of giving. You wait till I have written that letter. Cousin Mahlmann will be in tears when she reads it and will beg you to come in and make yourself at home. I have other relations in the Rhineland, but there you might get mixed up in the fighting. I think Mecklenburg is the safest place at the moment. Gadebusch is a small village, they have plenty to eat and there won't be any bombing."

She immediately sat down and wrote to her country cousin, chuckling as she concocted imaginative inventions about our fictitious past and her great friendship with my mother in Kattowitz. She gave us the letter; with tears in her eyes she wished us luck and asked us to remember her after the war should she still be alive.

Margaret was on night duty in a hospital and soon left after an early supper. She promised to find out what time the train left for Mecklenburg the next day, and warned us not to open the door to anyone or to answer the telephone while she was away at work. Everybody knew she was working and any callers might be spies or Gestapo. We went to bed after she was gone, read for a while and slept. For the second night there was no air raid. Margaret said at breakfast the following morning, "I wish you didn't have to leave. You brought me luck. We haven't had a single night without bombing for ages. The Allies must know you are here and are sparing you."

She packed some clothes for us, made sandwiches, gave us some of our money she had in safe keeping and took us to the station. We protested, thinking she must be tired after a long night on duty, but she insisted, "I would not have a moment's peace if I did not see you onto the right train."

Chapter 18

A few hours later we arrived at the little station of Gadebusch. Charlotte had sent her cousin a telegram and she was expecting us. But Charlotte had been over-optimistic when she thought Frau Mahlmann would beg us to enter her house; she took us in very grudgingly. She was, so far, the only woman in the village who had not yet been allotted a family of refugees and would have to take some in sooner or later. She commanded her little daughter to show us to an attic room.

The stout, gruff, ugly woman did not have the slightest family resemblance to her pretty cousin in Berlin, nor did she know Charlotte's compassion and will to help. Her first question was, what were we prepared to pay for board and lodging. She fixed a rather steep rent and we paid for three months in advance. Not entirely dependent on charity, we felt better for having paid.

It was no pleasure living with the Mahlmanns. From the day we arrived until the day of liberation, no mealtime passed but that we got a lecture on the glorious Hitler regime. The woman was sure the leader had a trump card up his sleeve as well as a secret weapon and that it would just be a matter of time until the tide turned and the war was won. She never lost her firm faith in victory until the Americans actually took over. She made it quite clear that, in her opinion, refugees were foreigners wherever they came from, and that they would be deported once the war was over.

Frau Mahlmann's unfriendly attitude was heartily supported by her older daughter, a plain, ardent Hitler Youth member, and by her oldest boy, a precocious ten year old. Both made us feel uncomfortable and often afraid when they added their pinpricks to their mother's open hostility. The father was away, a soldier at the Russian front, and the only one of the family who was consistently kind and thoughtful was the little girl who had first shown us to our room. She feared her mother's and sister's vindictiveness and had enough imagination to suffer with the homeless and displaced. She was only eleven years old, but she asked us more than once, "Why doesn't mother understand that it could happen to us tomorrow? If we were driven out of our village, wouldn't she hope for people to be kind and helpful?" She asked many questions we tried to answer as truthfully as possible without giving ourselves away.

The child was suffering under the treatment we received from her family, and to make up for it she introduced us to their neighbors, the Schlees, a kindly old couple, too wise to believe in the myth of a secret weapon. The old man, conscripted into the Home Guard, was put in charge of French and Italian prisoners who worked in a preserve factory next door. His prisoners had a wonderful life. His wife cooked for them and looked after them like sons. Except at night; they were not locked up, and I often met them strolling through the nearby woods. None ever attempted escape for they knew that would cost old man Schlee his job if not his life. They adored him and his wife and were quite content to sit out the war with them.

It was this old gentleman who warned me one day in February that all refugee girls under twenty-five were to be mobilized to join one of the German fighting forces unless they had regular and essential employment. He quickly found me a job before anybody else in the village knew of the recruitment drive. He arranged with the foreman of the jam and preserve factory for me to work with the prisoners because, as it turned out, I was the only person in the village who spoke French.

The foreman was delighted at first as he could not get the prisoners to do their work properly, presumably because they did not understand what he told them about the machines. However, I soon got into trouble with him because I would not translate his foul language, his continual threats, and his lectures on Nazi doctrine.

He threatened to have me before a disciplinary committee of the Party, to have me thrown into a concentration camp, or sent to the Russian front. He didn't know, of course, that I had already been there and back again.

One day he hauled me before the boss for disobeying his orders and for assisting the prisoners in their "sabotage." The head of the factory was an understanding and more enlightened man. When the foreman had left the office, still raving at me as he went out of the door, he said kindly, "Look here, Miss Doverg, I am perfectly satisfied with your work and I shall prevent the foreman from taking you before a Nazi committee, but why don't you try to fool the crazy blighter a little while longer? Pretend to translate anything he says. He wouldn't know if you repeated the words "honey bunch" a hundred times in French. In a few weeks the war will be finished. You are too young to fall by the wayside at the eleventh hour." I took his advice, pretended to translate, and the foreman was satisfied.

And so we waited for the end of the war. My mother helped in the Mahlmann household as much as she could, but as she never could please Frau Mahlmann, she spent more and more time with the Schlees, helping Frau Schlee to mend the prisoners' socks and wash their clothes. In the factory, I got two proposals of marriage from a French and an Italian prisoner, who were hurt and blamed each other when I politely but firmly turned them down.

No more news came from the capital. Charlotte had

written regularly, but now her letters stopped. Berlin was under siege and soon we heard the rumbling approach of the front line. April was nearly at an end. Spring had come early that year. The sun was hot and everybody wore summer dresses. Our long-sleeved sweaters became conspicuous, but we didn't dare leave them off because of the tattooed numbers on our arms. Frequently now the Mahlmanns asked if we didn't feel hot, and while the sweat was pouring down our necks, we pretended to shiver and said we always felt cold.

I forgot one day and rolled up my sleeves to wash my hands in the kitchen. Fortunately, only the little girl was there, but she was observant and immediately asked what the number on my arm stood for. I was terrified but answered quickly, "Poppet, can you keep a secret? Promise not to tell your family?" She nodded. "Well, when I was a little girl, I ran away with gypsies and they tattooed this number on my arm so that I'd be one of their family because they all had numbers. My mummy fetched me back, but to this day she can't bear to be reminded of it because she was so terribly upset when I had vanished. That's why I asked you not to talk about it. Your family would never let her forget it and they would make my mother cry again."

The child said she understood perfectly and she would never do or say anything that would hurt Aunty Liz; she loved her far better than her own mother. I worried for a while but I needn't have. That child could keep a secret and she never mentioned what she had seen to a soul.

On the second day of May, old man Schlee was sent to the Western front to fight. It was only a few miles away. "What," he said, "leave the wife in charge of all these prisoners? I'm blowed if I'll go fighting at my age. Why don't they send that young gutter-snipe of a foreman? He managed to keep out of the war successfully." The old man was well over seventy and had lost two sons in Russia. He told the factory foreman what he thought of fighting a lost war at his time of life. The foreman was furious. Had the Allied troops been delayed, this bit of plain speaking would have cost Schlee his life. But nothing now could stop the German defeat. There was no opposition left in this part of the country. Old men like Schlee and young children were expected to hold back the mighty surge of the victorious armies. They were overrun, often without a shot being fired.

On May 5, 1945, early in the morning, the youngest Mahlmann children rushed into the house, out of breath and full of excitement. "The Americans are here! They are marching through the village!"

Already the one main street was echoing with the noise of tanks, armored cars, jeeps and marching feet. We hung out of the windows, eager to get a first glimpse of our liberators.

"Aren't you ashamed of yourselves to be seen looking at our enemies?" asked Mother Mahlmann angrily. She pulled her two daughters from the window and tried to get my mother and me away too. I turned on her at last.

"They may be your enemies. They are not ours. Leave us alone." My blazing eyes must have intimidated her. She asked no questions.

The first Americans passed under our window and we waved and shouted with joy. They waved back. So that was what a victorious army looked like. Sunburned and dusty, heads high and backs straight, an expression of pride on their faces that I'll never forget as long as I live.

With dismay I suddenly discovered the young Mahlmann boy aiming a shotgun out of the next window. Pushing my mother aside, I flew at him, hit the gun from his hands and slapped his round childish face hard. His mother gathered her howling offspring in her arms and screamed at me, "What do you think you are doing, you traitor? You wait till we have chased those bastards out of Gadebusch. I'll see you hanged for this! Get out of my house!" The younger girl tried to calm her mother but got only abuse for her efforts.

"Don't worry, Frau Mahlmann, we are getting out of your house now. We had no intention of staying longer than we absolutely had to." I pulled off my sweater and showed her the tattoo on my arm. "My mother and I are escaped prisoners from Auschwitz concentration camp, if that name means anything to you. I'm sorry we had to deceive you, but for us it was a matter of life or death."

The woman turned ashen and trembled. For the first time since we had come to her house she was speechless and frightened. Her little daughter threw her arms round my mother's neck and cried bitterly, "Auntie Liz, you poor, poor Auntie Liz! What have they done to you?" She hid her head in my mother's arm. "Whatever happens, I'll always love you. Will you take me with you if you have to go? I don't want you to leave." My mother gently stroked the child's long, fair hair as I went out of the door into the glorious, warm May morning.

Even before the victory parade was over, a civil administration had been set up in the mayor's office. The armed guards outside did not stop me. The number on my arm opened all doors for me now. Within minutes I was taken to the new town-major's office and got a royal welcome when I revealed my true identity.

"Haven't you grown since I saw you last. You are a woman now and a lovely one at that," the major said in perfect German. I thought for a moment he had gone crazy or, later, that he had mistaken me for somebody else. Neither was true. He had, in fact, gone from Berlin to America when Hitler came to power. The son of a well-known Christian family, he had befriended my oldest brother at

Heidelberg university. He had known my parents well and me as a small child. Our world had become a small place.

Busy though he was setting up his administration, he immediately delegated his duties to a subordinate, packed me into a jeep and drove to the Mahlmann's house to see my mother. They had a long talk, and in the end the major asked if I would care to join their intelligence corps as an interpreter.

"We have a big job ahead of us hunting down SS who are presumably hiding in this neighborhood. You could be of tremendous help, if you would." He almost pleaded. Why, wasn't this what I had dreamed of and waited for all these years? I just nodded. "Can you come with me now?" he asked. My mother's serene, happy face made the sun seem brighter.

Frau Mahlmann had stood by all this time trembling. She did not understand English and had no idea what we were talking about. The major now turned on her and said in German, "Until we find better accommodation for Elizabeth and her daughter, you will give them your best rooms. If you fail to obey my orders, I shall have you and your family evacuated. Is that understood?" The woman promised to make us comfortable and apologized for her early morning temper. But my mother refused and said we were perfectly happy in the attic in the meantime. She need not move out of her rooms. The major frowned. "You are too soft with these people, Elizabeth, but have it your own way."

"Come along then, Daniella, we have a lot of work to do." First we went to the Schlees to free the French and Italian prisoners. They embraced the major, who was somewhat bewildered by the many kisses he got on both cheeks in typically Latin fashion. He told the men they could go anywhere they liked, of course, but it would take a little while and some organization to get them repatriated. Asked what kind of treatment they had received, they had nothing but good to say for their warden and his wife. Therefore the Schlees were instructed to continue looking after their charges until they could be sent home.

We returned to the major's office where I got my own desk, and for days sifted and translated intelligence reports. A few Jewish officers were attached to our unit and they treated me as though I were highly breakable porcelain. I was not allowed to walk alone anywhere. Wherever I went, at least two guards trailed behind. Guards were placed in front of the Mahlmann house and I was given a jeep for my own use. Every afternoon after work, I was taken home and a few officers and some of the ex-prisoners invariably assembled in the house to chat with my mother and me. We received American rations, chocolate, cigarettes and clothes.

My family was informed of our survival and my cousin, who was an officer in the U.S. forces stationed in Bavaria, was rushed to Mecklenburg to see us. The tremendous pile of work on my desk stopped me from thinking too much, and the consideration, kindness and respect we received from the occupation forces was heartwarming. For the time being, I was contented and almost purring under the unaccustomed freedom and friendship we were given.

Reports of SS hiding in the forests near our village began to trickle in and office routine was interrupted. I was bundled into a jeep and off we went on an exciting hunt. Many a time it turned out to be a wild goose chase, but often we were successful in tracking down individuals or groups of straying SS. What a despicable lot they were. Cringing, subservient, begging for their lives, they were a far cry from the vain, strutting tormentors we had known in Auschwitz. The clock had turned full circle. Now I was no longer the hunted but the hunter. I felt all the glory of freedom and revenge, until one day the difference between us and our ex-masters was brought home forcefully.

Two captains, a lieutenant of the 7th American Army Intelligence Corps and myself were combing the woods for SS who had been reported in the vicinity. Some SS women were said to be with them. Troops were covering every move we made.

At the age of twenty-three, I was still young enough to thoroughly enjoy the exhilaration of the chase. The new town-major had tried to stop me from taking part in these manhunts, but I felt I had survived for this and that I deserved the satisfaction of catching at least some of our murderers. The Jewish captain under whose direct command I now worked, managed to persuade the major that my presence was justified when arrests were made. The major acquiesced. Actually, there was little danger involved. Not one of the cornered heroes tried to shoot it out; probably they had run out of ammunition long ago. Mostly they had thrown their revolvers away before they were captured.

For hours we patiently covered every inch of the woods and had almost given up hope, when somewhere above our heads a branch cracked and broke. My captain jumped back and pulled me behind a huge oak tree for cover. Like an overripe plum, a woman dropped to the soft mattress of dead leaves. She wore the dreaded grey uniform of women guards, minus her revolver belt. She tried to break away and run, but before she moved more than a few yards, the captain and two soldiers pinned her down, turned her towards me and asked me if I had seen her before. Had I seen her before! She was the woman who had begged for our help when she thought Auschwitz was about to be taken over by the Russians and who had kicked my mother down the stairs as soon as she had orders to

evacuate us. I told the captain of that incident an
had hoped to meet her again after the war.

The SS woman whined and cringed and insisted she
had never heard of a place called Auschwitz. The captain
turned her over to a couple of guards and instructed them
to take her to my office. Without being asked, the woman
revealed the hiding places of five SS men and another two
women before she was led away. We picked them up on
the way back to the village.

In the woman's pocket were found photographs of
the entrance gate to Auschwitz and pictures of a hanging.
She said she had never seen these pictures before. Somebody must have planted them on her. The tall guards
brought her into my office and then stood outside the door.
The captain opened a desk drawer, pointed at a small
revolver in there, put his hand on my shoulder and said
quietly, "For your protection. She is all yours. Do you
want me to stay?" I shook my head and he too went outside.

The woman continued to deny she had ever seen
Auschwitz. I showed her the number on my arm and she
turned a pasty grey. I reminded her of the day of our eva-
cuation, of her breaking her whip after taking the clothes
off the prisoners and leaving them standing half-naked in
the snow. I reminded her of the broomstick she had beaten
us with when the order to evacuate had come through.

She slumped forward against my desk, tears streaming down her face. She pleaded for her life; she offered me
money, a house, anything I would ask for, and she was a
disgusting sight. I picked up the revolver. How often had I
promised myself to kill her? In those early days immediately after the war there was a time of rough justice.
Nobody would have turned a hair if the revolver had gone
off and an SS woman had been shot. For a moment I aimed
the weapon at her. It was impossible. I could not kill in

cold blood, not even a murderess.

I slipped the revolver back into the drawer and got up. The woman whined and bubbled out a full confession and the captain, who had quietly come in again, took it all down. Still she continued to plead with me to let her go. She had not missed my weakness and was leaning hopefully on my desk. Recoiling with disgust at her and myself, I shouted at last, "Stand up, don't touch that desk or anything else I come in contact with!" She shrunk back into a corner and the captain called for guards to take her away. She did not escape. On her own confession of all the murders she had committed, she was hanged shortly afterwards.

Two weeks after this encounter, our work in Gadebusch was finished; the civil administration worked smoothly and we were posted to a larger town. A jeep took my mother and me to a delightful house that had been requisitioned for us. The brigadier in charge was there to welcome us. He handed the house keys to my mother, invited us for dinner, and left. My mother opened the door, we went inside and gasped. The sun was pouring in the windows. In every room were huge bowls of white and purple lilacs and the whole house was permeated with the lovely scent. Everything we could possibly want was in the house. There were cigarettes and chocolates, a bottle of wine and glasses on the table. In the bedrooms, both our dressing tables were loaded with perfume and cosmetics. The larder and kitchen were well stocked. In the bathroom we found scented soap, bath crystals and soft, white towels.

I stood at the window gazing out into the sunny garden with its flowering shrubs and spring flowers.

"This is what I have wished for you, my Daniella. My dream has come true," my mother said softly. "You are young enough to start a new life and be happy again. This beauty is only an interim. You will not always be spoiled and treated with so much consideration. But I could not think of a lovelier springboard for a new start or for a better place to rest for a while. If ever you look back in despair, remember this day and remember that, in the end, there were, after all, people who fought for us. There will be a new generation happy to be alive who will, I hope, never know the horrors we have seen. If we have one mission in life, a debt to all who have died, you will carry it out. You, Daniella, will see to it that young people will not ever again be persecuted for their race, color, or beliefs."

"Yes, Mother, I'll try," was all I could say. But it sounded hollow, skeptical and without conviction. Yet, when I realized her need to relinquish at last the burden of responsibility, I knew I had to take over where my mother had left off. Her superhuman strength had saved my own and other lives over and over again. Now it was my turn to repay the love and sacrifices I had taken for granted. That day so long ago, I promised my mother, my murdered little family, our six million dead, and myself that, never again, as long as I lived, would a dictatorship rob our children of their birthright, their freedom and their happiness.

Epilogue

by Andrew Ogle

The southern Alberta village of Coutts is home to about four hundred souls and would be considered unremarkable by most travellers except that it is a major border crossing into the United States. The village is one more slight bump on the vast prairie landscape—grain elevators, a small oasis of houses and trees surrounded by miles and miles of rolling wheat fields. To the east rise the Sweetgrass Hills, and just over the western horizon are the majestic Rocky Mountains.

Motorists heading south into the United States reach the border checkpoints almost before realizing they are in a village. Just before the Canadian customs and immigration buildings is one last village street, newly paved like all the others. Because there are innumerable customs brokers' offices there, it is usual to find several trucks parked on the street. One block west up the street is a small park, and then the village's two-storey brick elementary school. Another couple of blocks of houses line the street and then the open prairie takes over again. Among the houses is a small, yellow bungalow, its front yard surrounded by a high hedge of Russian Olive, sheltering a variety of flowers.

Here, a world away from the horrors of the Holocaust, lives Eva Brewster—Daniella Raphael. She's a grandmother now, and a busy one, writing a column for weekly papers that for years was published by the daily newspaper in Lethbridge, a city of about 60,000 people 100 kilometers to the north. Newly elected to the local council, she tended house for her husband Ross, a federal agriculture department border veterinarian, until his recent death. She is an inveterate traveller, journeying often to Israel where her mother, now in her eighties, lives on one of the country's first kibbutzim.

Just as the Holocaust seems a lifetime removed, so too was Eva-Daniella's childhood in pre-war Berlin a world away from the horror that was to come. Her forbears had lived in Berlin since the twelfth century and her father came from an independently wealthy family whose fortune went back to the time of Frederick the Great. Eva was born near the end of the terrible inflation after the First World War. "My family always claimed that my complete indifference to worldly goods stems from that time," she says. "They used to give me million mark notes to play with, and according to them I broke into fits of laughter every time the wind carried them over the balcony of our apartment."

Eva's mother was a good deal younger than her father. They married when she was nineteen and he was thirty-eight. It was his second marriage. His first wife died during the flu epidemic after the First World War, leaving him with three young children, aged about four, ten and eleven at the time of his second marriage. After Eva, the couple had one other child, a son.

Eva's memories of her childhood evoke a picture of an enchanted time. Her father was the owner of one of the largest import-export firms dealing in foodstuffs in Berlin; the family lived in a fourteen-room apartment and had a summer house by one of the lakes near Berlin. There were holidays all over Europe, to Czechoslovakia and Switzerland in winter for skiing, and Denmark in summer where the young Eva swam in the North Sea for hours at a time, dreaming of breaking the cross-channel swimming record. Berlin itself had beautiful parks, the Tier-Garten (Animal

Garden), the zoo, a forest and lakes within cycling distance of her home, skating rinks in winter, aquariums, terrariums, theatre, opera.

But the storm clouds were already gathering. "When Hitler first began to spout forth in public," Eva recalls, "my father dismissed him as an uneducated propagandist. Germany, he predicted, would never fall for him. At that time I was eleven and my brother was ten. We listened to Hitler's ravings and couldn't stop laughing. If we had read *Mein Kampf,* we would have expected the anti-Semitism that was already becoming apparent, but none of us had."

When Hitler came to power in 1933, Eva's father was warned by friends who had joined the Nazi party to take his money and his children and get out. But with his age and position, he simply did not want to leave, and refused to believe what he was told. He was an officer in the First World War, his brother fell in the front line and so did innumerable other members of his family. He was born a German, his family had been in Germany since the twelfth century, and that was that.

But Eva's stepbrother, who studied law at the University of Heidelberg, saw the beginning of anti-Semitism there and left Germany for Palestine in 1933. Her youngest stepsister, who was sixteen in 1933, soon followed. Her other stepsister, a high-calibre athlete, was supposed to take part in the 1936 Olympics. Just before the Games started, a story was put out in the newspapers that she had broken her leg and couldn't compete. Actually, she was under house arrest under threat of imprisonment. Eventually she married and left the country with her husband on one of the refugee ships bound for South America that was refused entry at every port it reached. Finally they escaped in Uruguay.

On January 26, 1938, Eva's father died of a heart attack. "That day," Eva remembers, "he had been 'invited' to have dinner with the Minister of Agriculture who informed him that a new law soon to come into force would require all Jewish businesses to be handed over to Aryans. The Jews could not set a price for their businesses but were presumably to get the value of whatever they owned. That money of course never materialized. Anyway, my father was told that night he could not go back to his business and the next week somebody else would be taking it over. That night he died.

"After my father's death, my mother very quickly sent my brother to Sweden to a boarding school. I was supposed to go with him but I just couldn't face it. In spite of everything, perhaps my parents protected us too much and didn't tell us all they knew and perhaps I still didn't take it seriously. I said I would go if my mother would go, but she had taken up nursing by then and wanted to finish her training. By that time the first concentration camp inmates had been released, those who had got visas through relatives to go to Britain or America. They were in such shocking condition my mother felt she was needed in the hospital to nurse them back to health because they weren't allowed out of the country until they had recovered."

Later, Eva tried to get a visa, but most doors were closed. Finally she got one for South America through her stepsister but was not allowed to travel there on her own. The German authorities claimed there was still white slavery in South American ports. They could not accept responsibility for sending a sixteen-year-old girl there "unchaperoned." Later, when the Nazis were sending much younger girls to the gas chambers, such an excuse would seem incredible. Nevertheless, at that time Eva was told it would be different if she were married. And that was one of the reasons for her marriage at sixteen to a boy she had fallen in love with at twelve, the ill-fated Freddy Raphael. But by then Germany had invaded Poland and it was too late.

Eva's memories of the pre-war period are as vivid as her telling of the terrors of Auschwitz. But there are physical reminders as well: fading photographs of her first husband and of herself and her mother with Reha. Of the concentration camp experience there remains a small scar on her arm where the hated tattooed camp number had been before she had it removed. Below, the scar, the triangle, indicating her camp status as a political prisoner, is still there. It has been a long time since Eva and her mother escaped the Nazi terror. Eva has had a full life; she remarried, had two more children and lived in Africa, England and Scotland before coming to Southern Alberta.

When the war ended in Europe, the American 7th Army, which Eva had been working with, was posted to Japan, and Eva and her mother were transferred to Lueneburg, an ancient town near Hanover in the then British-occupied sector of northwest Germany. On the personal recommendation of her American superior officer, Eva was employed as an interpreter with the British Control Commission. Her mother immediately started work as a nurse in the large, understaffed hospital for refugees.

Only a few weeks later, Otto appeared at their apartment. He had been given their address by the Swedish Red Cross where known survivors were registered. By then Otto was already the respected mayor of a large East German city. Now he asked Eva to marry him.

"He offered my mother and me a wonderful home, love, peace, and most tempting of all, life in what he believed to be the best of all worlds, a just and incorruptible society. He left alone and heartbroken. Even if I had loved him as a man rather than a father figure, I could not voluntarily have joined him in Russian-occupied East Germany and so exchange the dictatorship we had just escaped from for another.

"Not long after Otto had returned to his city, his best friend escaped to the west and brought us a last message. Otto had been arrested and deported to Siberia. A man whose main mistakes were to trust a system that thrives on suspicions and denunciations and to love his country and fellow Germans in spite of what they had done to him, refused to escape with his friend through the back door of his home while the Russian secret police broke down the front door. He was still convinced he could persuade the Russian leadership to ease its harsh regime and postpone war reparations until he had rebuilt his city's industries to be able to pay its debts.

"The population in his totally bombed-out city was starving. Yet the Russians requisitioned the very first post-war harvest for shipment to the Soviet Union. In despair, the mayor did what he had learned to do for survival as a prisoner of the Nazis—deeds for which the Russians had actually honored him and appointed him mayor. He unhitched an unguarded train already loaded with flour and destined for Russia, and in the middle of the night had it distributed to his hungry people. A high-ranking Nazi, who had much to gain from collaborating with the Soviets, denounced him. Otto was never heard of again."

Susan, who had been such a support to Eva in the camp and who had helped Eva and her mother escape from the train transporting the survivors of Auschwitz to Belsen, also survived. She and another ex-prisoner visited Eva and her mother in Lueneburg. The two girls later went to the United States, and, say's Eva, "we lost touch."

On April 1, 1947 Eva married Ross Brewster, a Scot she met in Germany while he was with British intelligence forces. After demobilization, they returned to Scotland where Ross resumed his veterinarian studies interrupted by the war. He had always wanted to go to Africa, but on graduation a friend persuaded him to help out with his practice in Devon which had grown too large for him to manage alone. However, after a few years, during which he got busier and busier, Ross decided he had had enough and called up the colonial office to say he was ready for his first African assignment. By this time, Eva was pregnant and a daughter was born in January, 1953. Scarcely two and a half months later, Ross left for Nigeria and Eva for Italy, where she was to stay with an aunt until Ross found suitable living quarters. As it turned out, Eva's stay in Italy was short lived.

"When I landed in Rome with my little daughter, the first people I met at the airport were two ex-officers that I had known in the American 7th Army. They were on their way to Israel. Soil experts, they had been sent by their government to study what had been done in Israel to combat erosion problems. Well, they more or less fell around my neck and said one of their number had fallen sick and how would I like to join them on their plane to Israel? So I didn't even unpack my daughter from her carry cot, sent a telegram to my aunt to say I was on my way to Israel, and landed in Tel Aviv the same day."

Eva's stay turned out to be eight months. Her husband was immediately posted to the bush after arriving in Lagos and worked in conditions too primitive to bring his family. They were reunited when he returned to Lagos. A second child, a boy, was born there in 1955. After two years in Lagos, the Brewsters were send to Vom, a research station in northern Nigeria. They spent two more years there and then it was off to the Cameroons, where Ross was appointed director of veterinarian services. In 1962, the Brewsters decided to return to England and went back to Devon, where Ross again set up a practice.

He was just getting his practice up to the point where

he was nearly as busy as he had been nine years before when a phone call came from his aunt and uncle in Scotland, north of Inverness, begging him to come and take over the family farm. They were getting too old to manage the farm that had been in the family for generations. Ross felt obliged to accept and the family moved again. However, the farm was really too large to run as a family farm. "Every one of our six hired men earned more than we did without having the planning and the weekend work," Eva remembers. After five years, the Brewsters gave up on the farm. Ross accepted an offer from the Canadian government and moved his family first to Edmonton and then, in 1970, to Coutts. "We sold the farm and found, two years later, that had we hung on a little longer we could have made a fortune because by then they had found oil. But we never thought about what if."

In a new home, in yet another new country, Eva began her writing career almost by accident. It began with a letter to the editor of *The Lethbridge Herald* about an incident that brought all the old memories of the war to the surface. A West German youth band taking part in the Calgary Stampede parade in 1971 played an old folk song that had been a favorite of the Nazis. Eva wrote that such a song was totally inappropriate. Her letter drew a storm of protest from the local German-Canadian community, mostly pointing out that the song had a long history in folklore and as such was not a "Nazi" song. Finally, the *Herald* publisher, Cleo Mowers, asked her to respond and conclude the debate. From that grew a weekly column that allowed Eva to express the strong views on democracy, individual rights and freedoms, intolerance, and racial prejudice that were shaped by those two years in Auschwitz.

She had occasion, for example, to write about the experience of her sister at the 1936 Olympics in connection with an Olympic boycott in 1972. She also wrote extensively about other subjects that interested her—the ongoing kibbutz experiment in Israel, the changes of the 60s and 70s, particularly as they affected young people, solar power, consumer issues, and, often, the need for people to participate in shaping the institutions that govern them and the decisions that affect them. Later Eva found she still had much to write about an all-too-familiar subject when the anti-Semitic teachings of an Eckville, Alberta, high-school teacher hit the national press.

An early result of her writing was that the Alberta government commissioned her to research and report on co-operatives in Israel. Her activities soon expanded to include writing and reading commentary for the CBC and independent television stations in Lethbridge. Later, she wrote, organized, and hosted a twelve-part television series with a studio audience question-and-answer period that earned the station an award for the best community program. That series was a follow-up to work Eva had done with young offenders, alcoholics and drug addicts in the Lethbridge Correctional Institute. She also contributed articles and photos to Alberta Teachers Association magazines and wrote and acted as a commentator in school broadcasts for social studies in Alberta Schools. Until 1981, she was a regular guest lecturer at the Lethbridge Community College journalism program. For such activities, she was chosen a "Ms. Chatelaine" in 1976 and a YWCA "Woman of the Year" in 1977. In 1986 she was awarded an honorary Doctor of Law degree from the University of Lethbridge in recognition of her writing and service to humanity. Eva considers much of her work as part of a "feeble attempt to keep my rash promise to my mother and a future generation. To this day, children and young people are my main 'hobby' and concern."

But, as with most columnists and commentators, not everyone has agreed with her point of view. "I have been criticized," she has written, "and accused of being hypersensitive to prejudice and of seeing dangers where none exist. I hope this book will explain to my critics why a seasoned, objective journalist would react so strongly to, for example, the suggestion made a few years ago in the Alberta legislature that prisoners and welfare recipients should be put to work at 'voluntary' labor in the southern beet fields. The objection that 'there might not be enough "volunteers" to fill a string of boxcars heading for labor camps in the South. . .' evoked in me nightmare memories that have to be shared to be understood."

One gets a sense in talking with Eva and in reading what she has written that she feels she has not succeeded in keeping her promise to her mother. Conditions around the world, including North America where "widespread intolerance is a reminder that dislike of those who are 'different' did not die with Hitler," indicate that the problems that led to the dictator's rise to power are repeating themselves. For a survivor, one of only seven of the one thousand in that transport of April 20, 1943 to honor the Fuhrer's birthday, such conditions have imposed a very personal imperative. It was this understanding that "persuaded me to relive a story that has haunted me for almost four decades. Having failed so miserably to keep my promise to a future generation, it is my last hope that this book may open the readers' eyes to the dangers they refuse to face up to."